My Kevin,
Thank you
for being such a good
friend, encourager, leader,
challenge, & lover. You are
my perfect Valentine – all year
'round. – I love you
– with all my heart.

Happy Valentine's day
– 1985 –
Forever, your Patty
XXXOOO

THE NEW
COMPLEAT
ANGLER

THE NEW COMPLEAT ANGLER

Stephen Downes

Illustrated by Martin Knowelden

Endorsed by the Izaak Walton League of America

STACKPOLE BOOKS

First published in Great Britain by
Orbis Publishing Limited, London
1983
© 1983 by Ruan Martin

Published by
STACKPOLE BOOKS
Cameron and Kelker Streets
P.O. Box 1831
Harrisburg, PA 17105

Phototypeset by Tradespools
Limited, Frome, Somerset.
Printed in Italy

Contents

**Library of Congress Cataloging in
Publication Data**

Downes, Stephen.
   The new compleat angler.

   l. Fishing   I. Title.
SH441.D68   1983   799.1'2   83–5009
ISBN 0–8117–1011–4

MORNING TROUT

Foreword

The eminent scientist Sir Isaac Newton wrote, "If I have been able to see a little farther, it is by standing on the shoulders of giants." All of us who have written about fishing and made, perhaps, one or two original contributions to that art, might say much the same; but this book is exceptional. Not only has the author chosen the right giants; he has surveyed wider horizons from their shoulders. At a time when books about angling are becoming more and more specialised and instructional, a new one that looks, and looks clearly, at the broad spectrum of fresh water fishing is not only welcome, it is needed.

It celebrates the ter-centenary of the death of Izaak Walton, who, for some reason, has come to be regarded as the Patron Saint of Angling. I have always found this reverence for Walton hard to understand, since nearly all of the contents of his *Compleat Angler* were filched from predecessors, among them Dame Juliana Berners, William Samuel and John Dennys, and served up with a sauce of preaching, unleavened by any trace of humour. Even if Walton had had all the advantages of the information that has become available since his time, I do not believe that he could have written nearly so good a book as *The New Compleat Angler*. I cannot, therefore, look on this book as commemorative, though its author, publishers and even the public may well do so. To me, it stands as a splendid contribution to angling literature in its own right. I find the word "scholarly" altogether inadequate to describe the standard of writing it contains, or the vast amount of reading and research that its author must have carried out in the course of producing it.

I know of no other book dealing with either fishing or fish, in which the author has been able to combine important biological information with an appreciation of the beauty of a creature, expressed in splendid prose, which, in places, is almost poetry. I shall not choose examples; let the reader discover them for himself, as a prospector might find nuggets in a gold field; in this case, a very rich gold field indeed. He will also, in the course of his search, find gems of information about fishes that will prove of immense value in his attempts to catch them in greater numbers or in larger sizes.

Earlier in this introduction, I spoke of the many modern fishing books devoted to a single species of fish or special methods of fishing, or to particular kinds of water. Most of these books are valuable, but there is not one that cannot be better understood and appreciated after reading *The New Compleat Angler*, which weaves so many rich threads of knowledge into a splendid tapestry.

It leaves me with a feeling of inadequacy in my own writings – as Shakespeare put it, "I am no orator, as Brutus is; But as you know me all, a plain, blunt man." I can therefore only in one plain, blunt word, describe this book as magnificent.

Richard Walker, Biggleswade 1983.

Introduction

Winchester Cathedral rises out of its green close, long, grey, square-cut, like a great stone ark run aground. In the flagstoned floor of Prior Silkstede's chapel lies a plain dark slab, out of reach of the low midwinter sun. "Here resteth the body of Mr Izaac Walton who died the 15th of December 1683 . . ."; and the epitaph records his ninety well-spent years. Above, the morning light pours through the window which the anglers of England and America gave to the cathedral of Winchester, a long lifetime ago in the summer of 1914, in memory of the author of the happiest of books. Walton in stained glass looks down from both corners; once seated among the meadow flowers beside the Itchen, below the chalk scarp of St Catherine's Hill, his rod laid aside and a book in his hand. "Study to be quiet" is inscribed below, his favourite text, which he placed at the end of *The Compleat Angler*, after Piscator's blessing on all that are lovers of virtue, and dare trust in providence, and be quiet, and go angling.

In the left corner Walton is seen kneeling beside the steep rocky banks of a stream that must be the Dove in Derbyshire; for a younger man, bearded, sits beside him, who from his look of respect for Walton and of mild surprise at finding himself commemorated in a church can only be Walton's friend Charles Cotton, remembered for his *Directions how to Angle for Trout and Grayling in a Clear Stream*, the worthy continuation of Walton's work. "In everything give thanks," says the window; and Cotton in his other writings was abundantly grateful for the pleasures of love, sherry and gambling, yet kept Walton's affection.

Above, in the central light of the window, "the Lord sitteth above the water flood": as Winchester cathedral itself rests above submerged waters, floating on a buried raft of elm-trunks; held up now through the efforts of William Walker, the diver, who saved the cathedral with his own hands, labouring for seven years in the flooded crypts. St Peter stands to the right, and the other apostolic fisherman St Andrew to the left: they hold a salmon and a basket of mackerel, which must seem the fish of paradise to men of Galilee. Beside them are St Anthony and St Wilfred; Anthony is preaching to three fishes, one possibly an eel. At the bottom of the window, between the arms of Stafford where he was born and Winchester where he died, is the dedication to the prince of anglers.

In the south transept, only six yards from Walton's grave, stands the memorial of a very different man: Bishop Samuel Wilberforce the enemy of evolution, Soapy Sam who asked whether Darwin claimed descent from the apes on his father's or his mother's side. His effigy levitates upon the hands of six aerodynamically implausible angels. Prudence, Fortitude, Faith and Justice surround him; even Victorian sculptors drew the line at Truth. I think Walton would have been delighted by the theory of evolution, the most marvellous of all the wonders of nature; and he would not have found it an obstacle to his faith. It strengthens the sense of humility to think that you and I and the

A typical selection of fish for Walton's table: perch, pike, trout and eel

Pope are all descended from a fish. But Walton would surely have been troubled by the timescale that geologists have deduced from the layered rocks, where years accumulate to meaningless vast totals. A world that started in 4004BC is humanly comprehensible, but a hundred million years and ten million seem just the same.

A German physicist, Manfred Eigen, once put time and evolution in proportion. Imagine that every year of real time took only a second; then a very long lifetime, say a hundred years, would cover three thousand million years of real time, which is all the time that there has been life on earth; and for most of that century the only living things were single-celled, bacteria and algae and so on. The first fossils of complex, many-celled animals were laid down, on Eigen's timescale, about eighteen years past; the age of reptiles ended a little over eighteen months ago; modern man has endured for eleven hours, as a hunter and fisher for all except the last two or three. Fishes are old; there have been a sort of fishes for twelve years; modern fishes for more than two years.

And on that reckoning Izaac Walton lived a minute and a half, and his mortal remains have lain in Winchester for five minutes; and for how much longer?

From the transept the long high-roofed nave leads to the western doors. All English cathedrals have something of the tribal sanctuary, with the regimental banners hanging in triumph and the stone and brass military memorials that record service, misfortune and occasional heroism: "aide-de-camp to general Adams at the siege of Bhurpore . . .", "who lost his life by the accidental explosion of the ship's magazine. . .", " shot by a fanatic at Peshawar on the 23rd March 1899. . .", "named for the honour of KCB, had he survived. . .", "married the Honble Frances, eldest daughter of Field Marshal Viscount Hardinge. . .": flotsam left by the receding tides of empire that have come and gone since Walton's day.

From the cathedral it is a short walk to the quiet meadows beside the clear waters of the Itchen, under Saint Catherine's hill. Private fishing, inevitably; something that Walton viewed with only partial content, to judge by his approving quotation: "there are some covetous, rigid persons, whose souls hold no sympathy with those of the innocent anglers, having either got to be lords of royalties, or owners of land adjoining to rivers, and these do, by some apted clownish nature and education for the purpose, insult and domineer over the innocent angler, beating him, breaking his rod, or at least taking it from him, and sometimes imprisoning his person as if he were a felon. Whereas a true-bred gentleman scorns those spider-like attempts, and will rather refresh a civil stranger at his table, than warn him from coming on his ground upon so innocent an occasion." But those were more spacious days; would Walton recognise anything in angling now?

Lines and reels are completely changed, and with his enquiring mind he would have relished the improvements. The old long rods survive only as roach-poles, curiously revived of late in carbon fibre; as miraculous to Walton as spun diamond, but once he recovered from his surprise he would have accepted its virtues for all rods, though I suspect he would still have preferred to cut his own saplings. As a member of the Company of Ironmongers, he would have felt no surprise on learning of the inferior imitation, Cardon Fiber, made of fibreglass painted black: all trades have their tricks; but he himself dealt uprightly. He quit London in 1646, judging the city no longer fit for honest men, and did not return; could there be a greater proof of character?

The quietness he desired, the contemplation that leads to clear vision, is still there for those who desire it; not always in the same places, with the bypass carrying a continual roar around St Catherine's Hill. But a man may hope to fish by quiet waters even in troubled times, like those which amazed Walton's world. (Across the river from St Catherine's Hill lie the earthworks of Oliver's Battery, from which a four days' bombardment broke down the old walls of Winchester and let the Parliamentary army in to despoil the cathedral.) *The Compleat Angler* has acquired a lustrous patina with the passing of the years; but it was written in a time as turbulent and confused as any since.

Angling produces excitement and peace at once: and also mystery. Not just the mysteries of skill, which no book can teach; the mystery of the world beneath the water, so close and so different; a metaphor for the hidden depths of the human spirit, dear to many poets, even to Charles Cotton in his more graceful moments:

> *Standing upon the margent of the main,*
> *Whilst the high boiling Tide came tumbling in,*
> *I felt my fluctuating thoughts maintain*
> *As great an Ocean, and as rude, within;*

As full of waves, of depths, and broken grounds
As that which daily laves her chalky bounds.

Walton found enchantment in the wonderful nature of fish, and their extraordinary lives; for any angler, an unremarkable patch of ground is transformed by an insignificant pond or stream that, beneath its surface, is another world, which we can never know as its inhabitants do, but which can with skill be interpreted. A modern poet wrote well of the craft of angling and the mysteries of fish:

I have waited with a long rod
and suddenly pulled a gold-and-greenish, lucent fish from below
and had him fly like a halo round my head,
lunging in the air on a line.

One does not usually think of D.H. Lawrence as an angler; but he was a Nottingham man, from a city famous for its fishing skills (and an early example of municipal public relations: originally, Snottingham.) He saw the otherness of fish most clearly in

a slim young pike, with smart fins
and grey-striped suit, a young cub of a pike,
slouching away below, half out of sight . . .

but watching closer
that motionless deadly motion
that unnatural barrel body, that long ghoul nose . . .
I left off hailing him.

I had made a mistake, I didn't know him,
this grey, monotonous soul in the water,
this intense individual in shadow,
fish-alive.

I didn't know his God.

But the strangeness of fish has been a lure to biologists; though they know no more than anyone else of what a fish's god might be, they can describe tolerably well some of the ways in which it experiences the world. And so this survey of the fish of Britain's fresh waters, three centuries after Walton's death, can tell more than he knew of the fish's sight and hearing and strange life; mysteries enough to give any angler food for contemplation as he waits beside the waters that are always changing, and always the same.

There is in Sicily, says Diodorus Siculus, a fountain called Acadine, in whose waters spurious writings sink, while trustworthy books float; I suspect all books on angling, even Walton's, would sink a little. This is a book of echoes; when I repeat fishermen's tales, I do not necessarily claim to believe them. Walton was undoubtedly in the right when he distinguished between "anglers, or very honest men".

A Fish like Ripe Grapes

The perch is the most colourful of the fish that swim in our waters; a good fish for a beginner, angler or artist, for the small perch is a voracious and indiscriminate feeder, one of the fishes that really can be caught by a boy with a worm on a bent pin without too much trouble or luck, and its shape and colouring are so distinctive that anyone who cannot make a recognisable likeness had better take up photography. Its name commemorates its striking appearance. Etymologists trace the word "perch" to the Sanskrit *prsnis*, spotted, and to the classical Greek *perkanos*, which means the dusky green that one sees in a bunch of ripening figs or grapes.

It is technically a coarse fish, a summer spawner, an inhabitant of still waters and of moderate streams; but when simply cooked it is as delicious as any game fish. Anglers perhaps undervalue the perch, since the small ones are too easy to catch and the large old ones too difficult. Three or four pounds is large by angling standards; perch do grow to around eight pounds but nobody has worked out how to take them – the freshwater perches of Europe, that is; the great perch of the Nile and Ganges, are another matter, well over a hundred pounds, and in Australia the Murray River cod is a perch of sorts, that grows to not much less and is taken with half a pound of raw mutton for bait.

I think it is the first dorsal fin, which bristles like the crest of a helmet, and the colourfulness, that make the perch seem a heraldic fish. Heraldic beasts are never meant as exact representations of the animals whose essential qualities they embody. There never was a living leopard as savage and heroic as the rampant beasts of the royal arms; but occasionally real animals capture some of the extravagant qualities of their heraldic archetypes. Greyhounds or red setters, for instance, could appear on any coat-of-arms without discord; and the perch, among freshwater fish, has something of the heraldic splendour and flamboyance that are caricatured in the sea-horse. Its great scooping mouth, the proud fin carried like a banner, the armoured coat of scales, its vigorous aggressiveness all contribute to this impression, and the rich and harmonious colouring strengthens it. The range of tints in a healthy perch is wonderful, though not quite consistent with the rules of heraldry that prescribe a strict alternation of metal and colour. Bluish brown on the front of the head, bronzed and gleaming over the gill-covers, its body is dark olive green with a bluish or brownish tinge along the back, lighter on the sides and blending into washed-out gold above the pearl-white belly; the sides are strikingly broken with darker vertical bars, five to nine in number; the spiny first dorsal fin grey, sometimes with a little violet, and with the leading spines almost black; the other fins are an inconspicuous yellowish green except for the red tail and the lower fins which are a brilliant orange or almost vermilion.

An old perch, leading a solitary existence, feeds off its own kind

Much of this beauty must be perceptible to the fish itself, as it looks back down its body or up into the mirror above it; though a literate perch might describe itself in other terms, for the perch's colour vision is very different from ours. It neglects blues and concentrates on reds, even on what to us seems colourless infra-red.

It is difficult enough to know how the world seems to another human being, let alone to another animal; and fish are very diverse, with far more striking differences in their modes of perception than can be found in mammals which share a relatively recent common ancestor. But by studying the visual pigments and apparatus of the eye, and by training fish in laboratory aquariums to respond to signals of different colours, physiologists conclude that all fish except those that have lost their eyes altogether can see some sorts of colours.

The retina, the layer of light-sensitive cells that lines the eyeball, onto which the lens focusses images, contains a mixture of rod and cone cells in fish as in men. The rods are far more sensitive but can produce no appearance of colour; night vision, all black, white and shades of grey even in silvery moonlight, depends on rods only. Cones need daylight brightness to stimulate them but discriminate between colours. Different types of cones absorb, and in absorbing are stimulated by, different colours of light, though no cone is sensitive to one colour only: a blue-preferring cone, for instance, will be slightly stimulated by blue's neighbours in the spectrum, green and violet. The range of colours seen, and the region of the spectrum where discrimination is most acute, vary between different species according to the colourings of the worlds that they, or their ancestors, lived in. Human eyes can see from short-wavelength violet to long-wavelength red but are most sensitive to, and discriminate best between, shades of green; a useful accomplishment for a monkey dwelling under a canopy of leaves. Fish live under very different lighting, and different fishes see different colours according to the waters around them: the perch's colour vision is extremely specialised to deal with the peculiarities of freshwater light, where red predominates.

The redness of light in fresh water may seem unlikely, for many expect it to be blue. Indeed, water by itself is blue, the clear deep blue of the sun-blessed Mediterranean or of high mountain lakes or of great oceans far from land. Other waters may seem blue if they reflect a blue sky (though no English writer seems to have noticed that the sea could be other than green or dark before Byron visited Greece); blue seas may change their appearance when reflecting clouds or the colours of sunrise or sunset (the evening Mediterranean can be Homer's wine-dark sea indeed, a deep bruised red), but beneath clear waters the light is always blue, since water itself absorbs blue light least. Red light is quite well absorbed by clear water, for all that it seems transparent when shallow; skin-divers who cut themselves - an occupational hazard for those attracted to wrecks and coral reefs - are surprised to see a green fluid flowing from their wounds when they are in no more than eighty feet of blue water, where the red light has vanished and the minor colours of the blood become apparent. Therefore fishes of the clear blue seas have many blue- and green-sensitive cones in their retinas, and few red-sensitive ones.

But water that is of any interest to anglers must be far from pure. Water alone cannot nourish fishes, or anything else. The Mediterranean and the deep tropic oceans are watery deserts, compared to the rich northern and southern seas which are green with the richness of algae floating in them; fish here swim in a dilute vegetable soup, and their retinas are specially sensitive to the green or yellow light that is best transmitted, or rather least well absorbed. Fresh waters are also green with algae, but if they flow through fertile land they are further coloured by the yellowish-red pigments of decaying vegetation, washed out of the soil by the rain. These reduce the underwater visibility still further, and absorb the blue green light even more than the water and the algae absorb the red; it is unusual to be able to see more than thirty feet even in relatively clear fresh water, but red objects stand out the most.

Therefore freshwater fish have colour vision biassed towards the red end of the spectrum, and choose red for conspicuous patches of colour; usually, as in the perch, these patches are on the underside where they can signal to other fishes underwater but will not be seen by predators on land or in the air – a defence evolved against herons and ospreys but now useful against anglers. Perch, which hunt very much by sight, have taken this red bias further than any other fish yet studied. Even their black-and-white rod-dependent vision is in a sense red-biassed; for the visual pigment in their rods is not rhodopsin, as in humans and all other mammals, but porphyropsin, a related compound which absorbs red light more strongly, and absorbs infra-red light to which rhodopsin is transparent. Many fish of fresh or brackish waters have mixtures of rhodopsin and porphyropsin in their retinas. Perch have pure porphyropsin, and of a kind which absorbs further into the infra-red than any other known pigment. And as for the cones which give colour vision, these too in perch have pigments based on porphyropsins; and there are no blue-sensitive cones.

Perch, and several other freshwater fish, even prevent blue light, such as penetrates to them, from reaching their retinas; for the cornea, the outer transparent portion of the eyeball through which light passes to the lens, absorbs blue light (but not green, yellow or red) and so in a living or freshly-caught perch appears to us to be a bright golden yellow. These corneas can be of use, incidentally, to careful purchasers at fishmongers and diners in fish restaurants; if you are allowed to choose the fish before it is cooked, check its eyes. Very fresh fish have clear or golden eyes; within a short while after death the eyes become red as blood seeps into them. In Naples, unscrupulous restaurateurs are believed to remove the eyes of fish past their first freshness and insert the unreddened eyes of newly-caught specimens, replacing the old eyes after the fish has passed the customer's inspection, with safety since all cooked eyeballs look alike. For this reason prudent and mistrustful Neapolitans – forgive the tautology – press the eye of the fish offered to them to see if it is firmly fixed.

*Small perch make excellent
sport with very light weight
tackle*

This rejection of blue light, as well as the specialisation in infra-red vision, is probably due to the cloudiness of fresh water as much as to its colour. Light passing through any medium is not just absorbed, it is scattered; large molecules and small particles can make light change its direction without being absorbed. Because of scattering, things seen in anything but the shallowest water have a misty appearance: sharp outlines are blurred, and underwater light, as in a fog or cloud, comes scattered from all directions, not just from the direction of the sun.

But short-wave blue light is scattered the most, and long-wave red the least; for short-wavelength light interacts with and is scattered by small particles that the longer wavelengths pass by. Photographers know that infra-red-sensitive film will give clear pictures of a scene that to normal eyes seems foggy, since the very long wavelengths of infra-red light pass through when all visible light is scattered. Eyes that depend on porphyropsins, then, can see clear infra-red colours through murky waters; and by using the yellow cornea to filter out the scattered blue, perch reduce the uniform background illumination.

When perch are trained to respond to flashing lights or to coloured patterns, they behave according to the predictions one would make from the structures of their eyes. A perch that has been trained to obtain food by pressing a lever marked with a white square, for instance, will respond to a lever that to human eyes looks uniformly white, but which has a square which selectively absorbs or reflects infra-red. And they are ten to fifteen times as sensitive to red or green signals as they are to blue;

yellow is perceived about half as well as red or green light of the same intensity, possibly because when neighbouring green- and red-preferring cones are stimulated at once by yellow they block each other's signals.

In fact, it is not clear that perch perceive blue as a separate colour at all; in theory they might be able to, despite their having no blue-sensitive cones. They could in principle deduce the presence of blue from the difference in stimulation of red- and green-sensitive cones; much as the human retina, which contains a mixture of blue-, green- and yellow-sensitive cones but has no cells that absorb preferentially in the red, senses red light from the difference in response of green- and yellow-preferring cells. This sort of system would allow the perch to devote as much of its retina as possible to red-sensitive cells that give it good penetrating vision, while keeping some range of colour discrimination, since a monochrome view of the world makes it easier for prey or enemies to hide.

All this is of more than physiological interest. The underwater scene as perceived by a perch must consist of outstandingly brilliant reds and oranges, with a multitude of different hues which to us seem identical and infra-red components which to us are invisible, standing out through a rather more foggy green-yellow haze. Now an angler trying to catch a perch needs a bait which will be conspicuously attractive to the perch, but baits are usually made as viewed by the human eye in air. For pulling in the small perch that hunt in packs, this is no problem; maggots or worms will do nicely, and the design is not in the angler's hands. But the big cautious perch that flourish in meres and lakes are another problem; apart from their logical but exasperating habit of lurking inextricably in weeds in summer and going down fifteen feet or more into the deeper, warmer water in winter, they respond poorly to most bait. Various standard coarse-fishing baits have been tried on them : large worms are sporadically attractive, minnows or such are sometimes acceptable livebait, spinners and spoons are imitations that deceive the occasional perch; but the big old ones are experienced – perch in aquaria have lived for twenty-seven years – and cunning. Few anglers have been able to report much consistent success.

The great Mr Richard Walker, tired of lowering rejected lobworms, designed the Hanningfield Lure specifically for large perch, and found it the most successful of all perch baits. It imitates, approximately, a small perch so as to attract the large cannibals; it is a tandem lure, one hook trailing, because perch snap at the tails of their prey; the body is of white wool ribbed with fine silver thread, the throat hackle and tail of hot orange cock-hackle, with a bunch of cobalt blue fibre overlying the hackle at the front; the underwing of closely-tied white goat hair, the overwing of turkey tail-feather; cheeks of small black feathers with white spots, head of varnished black silk. I am sure Mr Walker could make a more than adequate lure out of old matchboxes if he put his mind to it, but I cannot help wondering how much more effective a lure might not be made if it were designed specifically for the perch's idiosyncratic colour vision; if the perch sees anything of the cobalt blue, what the white wool and hair look like in the infra-red, and so on.

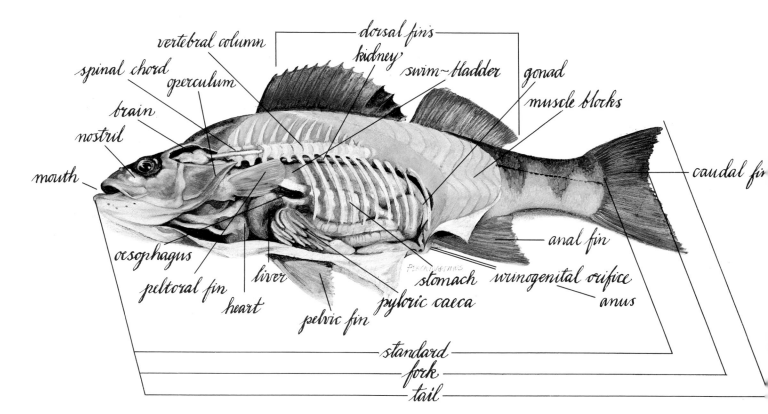

The anatomy of a freshwater fish

At any rate the principle of making an approximately striped bait to appeal to a perch is right, because a perch's stripes are another of its signalling devices. Patterns of light and dark stripes show up well through mist, as the designers of traffic warning signs are well aware. Underwater, a pattern of dark stripes is visible at about seventeen per cent greater distance than a solid black body of the size of the whole pattern. Coarse stripes are less affected by scatter than fine ones, and fishes' eyes do not resolve fine patterns well (another point to be borne in mind by the designers of lures).

Striped fish are probably signalling no more than "I am here", but some fishermen have thought otherwise. The most complex known message found on a fish was borne by the famous prophetic butterfly-fish of Zanzibar, whose dark tail had narrow curving white stripes that could be read, if taken as Arabic script, on the one side as "There is no God but Allah" and on the other as "A warning from Allah". The man who caught it was illiterate, and sold it in the market for a few pence; eventually it fetched five thousand rupees. With hindsight, since the memorable rule of Shaik Abeid Amani Karume after independence, one could congratulate any Zanzibari who fled from the omen.

I cannot omit to mention another informative fish which I read of, reported by two mediaeval rabbis who saw it from a ship sailing from Spain to Palestine. It was I forget how many hundred cubits long, swimming in great coils, encrusted with scales of purple and gold; it held its head clear of the water as it swam, and on its head was a crown, and between its eyes was written (I presume in Hebrew): "This least of all fishes is on its way to be Leviathan's breakfast."

I cannot say how such monsters might swim; the movement through the water of a mundane fish like the perch is hard enough for a terrestrial biped to understand. Their tactics when swimming are fairly intelligible; they are predators that, unless they are very large, hunt in shoals. Their prominent stripes and red fins can hardly conceal them from other fishes, but then their hunting tactics do not depend on concealment. They chase after and wear down prey much smaller than themselves; invertebrates when they are very small, fish for preference as they grow, perhaps almost exclusively fish when they are very large. Packs of moderate-sized perch will sometimes herd together shoals of small fry and then dash into the bunch to grab a victim; for these tactics, being conspicuous is probably an advantage.

Perch are not built for speed, but rely rather on a larger fish being always faster than a small one, and on their great manoeuverability. The fairly short and flattened body helps in this : it can easily bend sideways, being slender when viewed from above, but can be spun on its axis faster than a long slender cylindrical body of the same weight could turn. But this shape, inevitably, is less streamlined than a longer, rounded body, and limits the perch's speed.

The large fins, also, make for agility rather than forward speed. It is fairly obvious what the tail fin does : it, and the flattened body, push water backwards and so push the fish forwards. But the actions of the other fins are more complex, not at all like our use of arms and legs in swimming. Some of the fins of the perch have moved a long way from where they used to be, from where they were in the last common ancestor of fish and men. And also the operations of a fish's fins cannot really be understood without bearing in mind another relic of that common ancestry, the swim bladder.

It was in the Devonian period, a very long time ago, around four hundred million years (or twelve and a half years on Eigen's timescale), that freshwater fishes began to gulp air and wave their fins about; the first steps, for some of them, to becoming land animals. Fishes before that breathed only through their gills, and had nearly inflexible fins that could be moved only a little. Modern sharks still have these primitive fins, and can steer with them quite well as long as they are swimming fast and have a lot of water to turn in. This lack of agility is probably the reason for the absence, which anglers may deplore or welcome, of sharks from almost all fresh waters (not quite all; there are some in Lake Nicaragua). In shallow or enclosed waters more moveable fins are needed to give quick turning at low speeds; freshwater Devonian fish developed them, and also learned to swallow air and gulp it into bladders, originally outgrowths from their throats, from which they could absorb oxygen; presumably this helped them to survive in stagnant pools and summer droughts.

A few have stayed at this lungfish stage; some, with more jointed fins to start with, developed limbs with which they could crawl on land, and improved the air-bladder to form lungs; their descendants have gone on to conquer the land, the air and soon the stars. But there is an odd tendency in vertebrate evolution; animals that have become more or less adapted to life on land return to the water and profit by the features they have evolved while out of it. (Otter, seal and whale are at different stages along this path.) Some of the air-breathing fishes had fins supported by rays, that were unsuitable for evolving into legs; these fishes never got further out of the water than poking their snouts into the air, but even this gave them an advantage in the water. They have mostly kept the primitive lung; some still gulp air into it; but it has been converted into an air-filled swim-bladder, which gives neutral buoyancy so that the fish at rest neither sinks nor rises, and does not have to work to keep itself afloat.

These ray-finned fishes with swim-bladders have been the dominant freshwater and major marine vertebrates ever since their appearance. Most of the present-day ones, including the perch, are members of a group called the teleosts, in which the rays are connected by a flexible web of skin, and there is a complex array of muscles at the base of each fin that allows the fin to be swivelled about freely and also spread out, rippled or contracted; making them into most efficient steering and braking organs. Most teleosts have kept the four paired fins , pectoral before and pelvic in the rear, which were originally horizontal stabilisers and have become, in us, arms and legs; they have also the dorsal fins on the back and the anal fin below and behind, unpaired vertical stabilisers originally, to which we have no analogues. The tail ends, usually, in a similar rayed fin.

So much for ancestry; how does the assembly of fins work? The hydrodynamics of fish movement is incalculably complex; a crude but effective way of investigating the subject is to amputate some fins and see how the fish then perform. I have not been able to trace this technique back beyond Archdeacon Paley, the eighteenth-century theologian who compared the deduction of the existence of God from the complex order of the universe to the deduction of the existence of a watchmaker from the complexity of a watch. He was also a keen angler; his portrait in Oxford shows him in full canonical robes, with rod and line; and his conclusions about this fraction of the universe still stand, though fish fins are still experimentally removed to refine the details of our interpretations.

If the unpaired fins are amputated, a fish will remain upright in the water but finds it hard to swim in a straight line or to control its turning. This is clear enough: the vertical fins are stabilisers. But further, if both pectorals are removed, the head sinks; if both pectoral and pelvic fin are removed from one side, that side rises; if all fins are removed, or if the fish dies, it turns belly upwards.

The reason for this, which Paley never appreciated, is that the fish's posture depends on the balance between its weight and the lift from its airfilled swim-bladder. Now the swim-bladder in most fish is positioned in a way that would make a naval architect's hair stand on end, if he encountered a ship built on such principles; the centre of gravity is above the centre of thrust from the swim-bladder. The two forces are balanced, and as long as the fish remains perfectly vertical it is stable. But if it starts to tilt ever so little, it will turn over until the centre of gravity is stably below the centre of flotation. Constant small motions of the pectoral and pelvic fins counteract this tendency to capsize, and keep the fish upright.

This is indeed a lunatic design (Paley as a theologian would have been most uncomfortable had he understood it), if one thinks in terms of something like a ship which has crude and slowly-responding controls, and for which a capsize is usually an irreversible calamity. Recently, aircraft designers have realised that there is a great deal to be said for such constantly corrected instability, in a machine designed to change direction very quickly. Anything with the centre of gravity stably below the centre of lift resists attempts to tilt it over as it turns; stability is the enemy of manoeuverability. Therefore some modern fighters are deliberately built with the centres of gravity, thrust, drag and lift out of balance; no pilot can handle such an unstable machine, but it is now possible to install a computer which can calculate what is needed and make constant rapid adjustments to the control surfaces so as to keep the aircraft flying straight and level until the pilot decides to make a turn, when the inherent instability flips it over very quickly. Fish have benefited from extreme manoeuverability for a long while, as an alternative to being eaten; and they have an adequate on-board computer in their brain.

But the interactions between swim-bladder and fins are more complex than anything in an aircraft. The swim-bladder itself is in an unstable state; it changes its volume, and therefore the lift it produces, as the fish moves from one depth of water to another. Changes in water pressure with depth are surprisingly great; just rising from eight feet deep to the surface would make a swim-bladder expand by a fifth.

Fish can change the amount of gas in their bladders, though in the advanced types like perches that have lost the passage from the bladder to the throat this cannot be done quickly or comfortably, only by passing gases between the bladder and the bloodstream. This may be one reason why perch hooked at any significant depth try to stay there.

For when a perch changes its depth, it must compensate for the changed lift from its bladder with thrust from its fins, till its bladder volume is restored, if it is to remain at the new depth. Laboratory experiments with the fish swimming in pressurised tanks have shown that a perch that has its bladder air content adjusted to give neutral buoyancy at a depth of two metres can only just hold its position by swimming with its fins as it approaches the surface, and a perch adjusted to a depth of twenty metres can only hold its position at ten metres by putting its head down and swimming downwards with its tail, above that it is carried helplessly to the surface by its own increasing buoyancy. But there is no corresponding lower limit beneath which a fish will irresistibly sink, for even a contracted bladder must provide some lift and a fish can always swim enough to support the five per cent or so of its weight that is not buoyed up by the surrounding water.

When a perch is trying to keep still in the water it must also deal with another force unfamiliar to land creatures; the thrust from its own breathing. Fish take water in through their mouths and pass it out in a steady current over their gills; this backwards jet provides a small forwards thrust, so to keep stationary a fish must swim slowly

Zander will use any submerged cover they can find

backwards. This current from the gills may actually be used to help fish swim more efficiently; by dropping dye in the water in front of a fish you can trace the course of the water it takes in, and the coloured water leaving the gills flows in a smooth sleeve along the body of the fish, reducing turbulence.

And once a perch has started moving it may need to brake, or turn, quickly. The arrangement of the paired fins is particularly effective for braking. In more primitive fish they are low on the body and with the pelvic fins well behind, in the position from which amphibian limbs evolved; but in perches the pectoral fins have moved up to the midline of the body and the pelvic fins, analogous to our legs, have moved forwards till they are underneath the pectorals. Teleosts brake by spreading their pectoral fins and holding them out from the body, so as to generate a great deal of drag; if they are set low and held out squarely, the drag they create acts below the centre of inertia of the fish, tripping it up, as it were; and so a fish braking thus pitches head-downwards and starts to somersault as it stops. Primitive teleosts can counteract this by braking with their fins held at an angle to the flow of water, with the leading edges raised as in an aircraft's wings so as to generate lift as well as drag; when they do this they do not pitch, but the lift makes them rise in the water. But perch can brake smoothly by spreading out both pectoral and pelvic fins at once; the pectorals, high up level with the centre of inertia, create some upward lift as well as drag, but this is balanced by the downward thrust from the pelvic fins beneath them, which are held out at the opposite angle to the flow of water, trailing edge raised. A perch with amputated pelvic fins rises whenever it brakes.

This biplane arrangement of pectorals and pelvics is, as I said, a mark of modernity among teleosts; but far more primitive fishes once had it. In the Permian slates of England and Germany, formed from the sediments of two hundred and fifty million years ago, from the times before the dinosaurs, lie the fossils of *Dorypterus*, a five-inch fish with thick armoured scales. Clumsy though it may have been by modern standards, it had specialised in manoeuverability and had evolved the necessary shape: a deep, compressed body, high pectorals and pelvics moved well forwards. So much for apparent modernity.

The real mark of the modern order of fishes to which the perches belong is their spiny fins seen clearly in the first dorsal fin which the perch erects when threatened. These sharp bristling spines are a useful defence against many predators, though not against man; let us be grateful that they are not poisonous. They are in the dreaded weever, a small spiny-finned seafish whose venom causes such burning agony that fishermen who have mistakenly handled one have thrown themselves overboard rather than endure. (Injections of potassium permanganate solution are said to help, a scrap of information I hope never to need.) Apart from the weever and the stingray northern waters are free from stinging fish. I do not know why venomous species seem rare in temperate climates and common in the tropics; perhaps this is an illusion, and it is just that species of all sorts are more abundant in the tropics.

The spiny first dorsal fin is not just for defence. Perch fold it back for streamlining when swimming, but seem to use it for steering, raising it and swinging it over as they turn. They also steer with their paired fins, holding them out as brakes on the side towards which they turn.

A perch will use all these control surfaces to bring itself within biting range of its prey. It can bite even before it has quite caught up with small prey, for it has a protrusible mouth which can expand and shoot forwards, scooping up the victim which is carried backwards by the flow of water into the mouth cavity. This scooping motion is achieved by having a loosely-attached and double upper jawbone. The rear upper jaw, the maxilla, is hinged to the front of the skull only at its forward point, and then slopes backwards; the lower jaw is slung from the rear ends of each maxilla. You can covert yourself into a partial model of a perch's gape; clasp your hands together and hold them up in front of your face. Your body then represents the fish's skull; your shoulders are the attachment points of the left and right maxillae (your upper arms), and the lower jaw (your forearms and hands) is slung from your elbows. You can now shoot the apparatus up, out and back to make a splendid bite. But the perch can do even better; for though the lower jaw bears teeth, the maxilla does not. The upper teeth are carried on a separate forward upper jawbone, the premaxilla, which can slide forwards along the skull as the mouth gapes and increase the effectiveness of the bite. The perch will swim behind its prey in brief pursuit, then snap forward at its victim's tail to disable it if it cannot take it outright.

Now when a perch is offered a tempting morsel that conceals a hook, it will cast forwards its mouth at it and be readily taken; and the loss of one will not deter the next in the school. "They are like the wicked of this world, not afraid though their fellows and companions perish in their sight," a jest that was old before Walton. Long before Walton, too, they were esteemed on the table. But despite their delicious taste they are an unpopular fish among cooks, on account of their protruding, prickly scales which make them rough to handle, and which can be difficult to detach. There are various recipes for dealing with this problem; a Victorian one was to wrap a newly-caught perch, still wet, in three or four sheets of *The Times* newspaper, and bake it in the embers of a bankside fire. Charred paper and scales then peeled off together; but *The Times* has never been the same since they started printing news on the front page, and I would not guarantee its virtues nowadays. A reliable method is to grill the perch quickly, then to slip a knife behind its head and peel off the scales like a coat of mail. (This only works with very fresh perch, or with ones that have been gutted and scalded in boiling water that has been made acid with a little vinegar.) Serve with butter, salt and pepper to taste.

Oriental recipes for fish of the perch family are much more elaborate; the Chinese style is well worth tasting if you can find a suitable restaurant. They marinate the fish whole - one can detect mushrooms, onions, shrimps, sugar and soy in the sauce, but I expect I have failed to find the essential ingredients - and then steam it briefly so that the flesh

The perch is distinguished by its extending jawbones

remains sweet and firm. And in Calcutta there is a perch dish called "Cockup" of which I know only the name.

Perch is a wholesome as well as tasty food. Walton mentions a "stone" in its brain, unfortunately unknown to modern medicine, which foreign apothecaries prescribed against kidney-stones. And Fracastorius, a sixteenth-century physician, recommended perch as a diet for syphilitics; on what grounds I cannot say. I suppose that as a predator fairly high up the food chain it might accumulate mercury, which in those days was the only effective drug for such diseases, but the effect would surely be trivial. Massive doses of mercury are needed to be effective, with awkward side-effects. Eighteenth-century defendants were allowed to enter a "plea of salivation", to have their trial postponed, if the mercury they were being prescribed was making them drool so much that they could not intelligibly conduct their defence. A diet of perch might be temporarily preferable.

Perch, zander, pike, showing their different mouths. It is easy to see why the Americans call their sort of pike-perch "walleye"

Among the relatives of the perch, two breed in British freshwaters, the ruffe and the recently introduced pike-perch, otherwise known by its German name of zander: *Gymnocephalus cernuus* and *Stizostedion lucioperca*, to give them their scientific names, as prickly as they are.

But scientific classifications have their uses. The same plants or animals have different everyday names in different countries, and also different ones are sometimes known by the same name, and many obscure ones have no everyday name at all. To take an example just from English usage; "ruff" is also the name of a small seacoast bird, a kind of sandpiper; and the fish "ruffe" is sometimes known as "pope", an alias that is also given to the puffin and to the bullfinch. And names in very foreign languages are usually not so much ambiguous as unintelligible; who would guess that the Polish "szozupac" and Turkish "turnabaligi" are both the same fish, the English pike (or luce)?

International communication among biologists was therefore hazardous until in 1758 Carl von Linné (or Linnaeus) published his celebrated binominal system of nomenclature; he named the beasts and plants as no-one had since Adam. In his system each type of organism is given a two-part name; first the name of the genus to which it belongs, then the name of its species. A species is fairly easy to define as a breeding group; if two organisms can breed and produce fertile offspring they are in the same species. A genus is a group of species that a classifier believes are similar.

The name of genus and species are usually derived from classical words for, or descriptions of the organisms; not always obviously. "Gymnocephalus", for instance, means "naked head", not the most prominent feature of the ruffe; "cernuus" is "falling headlong, with the face towards the ground" which I suppose could be a description of its usual feeding posture. "Stizostedion lucioperca" is a source of confusion: the second word is formed by joining together good Latin words for pike and perch; the first is ambiguous Greek. I am inclined to think that "stizostedion" probably means "dapple-chested", which is a reasonable description of the fish's markings; but some biologists maintain that it means "pricked-breasted". That is grammatically possible, and might be a fair name for the nightingale that was supposed to thrust a thorn into her heart to spur her to song; how it applies to zander I cannot say. One authority, otherwise reliable, declares with neither grammar nor sense that "stizostedion" means "pungent-throated". Where no features are obvious, Linnaean names can be formed from the name of their discoverer or someone the discoverer wished to compliment; I forget who was the much-desired Caroline whose anagram became the names of the genera Cirolana, Nerocila, Conilera. . . .

Linnaeus died aphasic, unable to remember his own name or the words for common household objects, but before the inadequacies of his or any other human system for dealing with the bewildering variety of nature had become apparent. Species distinctions are a little artificial.

The ruffe is small, hard to find, but makes a splendidly durable live-bait

Among freshwater fish, it is hard to know whether two allegedly different species from different lakes or rivers, that will never meet in nature, can breed successfully or not. (The problem is worse with fossil species.)

But if species distinctions are a little blurred, no-one can really say what a genus is; "closely related species", but who is to judge closeness? And related genera can be grouped together into families; perches, ruffes, zander are all placed in the family Percidae, the perch-like fishes. Families are more or less obviously related, and so we can ascend through an increasingly complex and arbitrary series of groupings; families, suborders, orders, superorders, cohorts, infraclasses, subclasses, classes, superclasses . . . this classification works quite well for the land vertebrates among which men can make sensible intuitive distinctions.

Fish classification is less straightforward. Most modern bony fishes are placed in the "class" of teleosts, which contains a large number of types which are obviously all distinct in their skull and tail structure from more primitive classes of fish, and which can be reasonably grouped into families and orders whose relationship one to another is very far from clear.

Therefore different biologists have proposed very different high-level groupings. There is an irreconcilable opposition between "lumpers", who want as few groups and levels of groups as possible, and are happy with very large families, and "splitters" whose ideal is that each genus should contain two species at most, each family should have two genera, and so on. An ambiguously balanced judgement, perhaps, is that people are divided into two classes, those who divide people into two classes and the sensible ones. To make things worse there are different traditions even of specific and generic names. The zander, for example, was also classified as *Lucioperca lucioperca* (which avoids the *Stizostedion* quagmire). Taxonomists agree that the first published scientific name for a genus and species should be the correct one; naturalists sometimes ignore this.

A very few species and genera are wholly fictitious; *Ompax spatuloides*, an extraordinary Australian fish, long in the textbooks although only one specimen was ever seen, turned out to have been manufactured by the sportsmen of northern Queensland from the bill of a platypus, head of a lungfish, body of mullet and tail of eel, to give them entertainment during the visit of the distinguished Director of the Brisbane Museum.

To return from names to fish; the ruffe is the perch's smaller and rather less attractive cousin; similar in shape, except that the spiny first dorsal fin is fused with the second soft-rayed dorsal; very different in colour, obscurer, with fins only a little touched with red and with greenish-grey upper body and silver-grey belly. The first gill-cover bears a dozen small sharp spines; whence perhaps its name, after the starch frilled collars of former fashions.

At first it seems surprising that ruffe should happily inhabit the same waters as perch, without competition; for a small perch is remarkably like a large ruffe. They both breed in late spring and summer, the ruffe's spawning beginning a few weeks later; but the ruffe lays the eggs one at a time, adhering to the bottom, while the perch lays them in strings a yard long, sticking to plant stems. So the newly-hatched fry, which are perhaps most likely to compete with each other, start off in different parts of the water; and grown ruffe have specialised in bottom feeding as perch have not. Ruffe will probe their snouts quite deep into mud in search of odds and scraps, nearly as far as a carp will; perch, when driven to bottom-feeding by a lack of anything to chase, just peck at the surface.

Nevertheless, ruffe can be easily taken by float-fishing with fine tackle and red worms, or so it is said; few anglers would deliberately go in search of them nowadays, for all that Walton describes them as excellent table fare. Till the last century, though, the ruffe was sought out for a sort of antipathetic magic, on account of its other name of "pope"; anglers from Leeds and Sheffield and other Yorkshire towns used to meet at the aptly-named Crewel Bridge on the Trent in Lincolnshire, for the ceremony of "plugging the pope". They stuck corks onto the spines of all the ruffe they caught, and set them loose, free but unable to submerge, to drift floating down the river. It is not clear if the Pope became perceptibly worse, or indeed if the plugging was meant as more than an obscure gesture of contempt. "There are ten thousand brave fellows in this city," said Swift of the London of his day, "that will give the last of their blood in the cause of No Popery, and cannot say whether Popery be a man or a horse." We progress, slowly.

Another damned foreigner that was responsible for popular hysteria by the banks of the Trent is the zander, the most controversial of recently naturalised fish. Its other name, pike-perch, is genetically misleading (a hybrid between two such unrelated fish as pike and perch is quite impossible) but gives a good impression of its appearance; an elongated, fiercer-looking perch, with more prominent teeth, two very sharp conical ones at the tip of each jaw, without the bright fins and with more dappled markings. It grows much bigger than the perch, too, up to forty pounds in its European homes though none over eighteen have been taken here, yet.

The wisdom of importing the zander has been debated for some time. "It is said to be a desirable fish for naturalisation in British waters, but, " warned Sir Herbert Maxwell, as long ago as 1904, "although its flesh is of a high quality, the utmost discretion should be observed in distributing it; for it unites the omnivorous voracity and size of the pike with the defensive armature of the common perch. Such a formidable creature might work irremedial havoc if it became established in waters tenanted by other game fish." That learned and sporting baronet would have been even more admonitory if he had known that a zander lays its eggs a million at a time or more, as against the mere two hundred thousand that is the perch's best, with both parents guarding them till they hatch; and that, with its perch-like porphropsin-rich eyes giving it good vision in dark, murky waters, it complements the pike as a predator rather than competing with it. Pike like to lie in cover in clear water and dash at their prey; zander cruise more slowly through dark plant-free waters for choice.

Zander were nevertheless introduced early in this century, at first to the lakes of Woburn and Claydon; then in the sixties they were released into the waters of the Great Ouse Relief Channel, from which they have spread to neighbouring rivers. This was welcomed by the small band of zander enthusiasts, who appreciate having something to angle for in winter floodwater; less enthusiasm was felt by the majority of coarse anglers, who felt that roach and bream were meant for better things than zanderfodder. When a small, toothy, odd fish was found in the Trent, loud were the accusations against the Great Ouse River Authority; muted, but not retracted, when the suspect zander turned out to be a young smelt. In fact it is only a matter of time until zander spread into all lowland waters; therefore I will offer some consolation.

Firstly, it is its own worst enemy. Two small zander meeting head-on will each attempt to swallow the other; and I have seen a photograph of a chain of four of its close American cousin, the walleye, each having partly engulfed the one in front of it. Of the million eggs laid, how many are food for the others?

Secondly, big zander may not be as destructive as they look. Zander in laboratory tanks given access to roach of various sizes cull out the smaller ones; the food of choice for a mature zander is a roach no bigger than four inches. Also, zander specialists report excellent bags taken with dead-bait left lying on the bottom, better than the catches they can expect to make with live-bait; the fish, for all its fearsome appearance, is a scavenger as much as a predator. Zander have been taken with scales in their stomachs that must have come from bream bigger than themselves; but these were surely taken from fish already dead.

Thirdly, it looks like an excellent subject for biological control. The Russian biologist Gintort, studying the fish of the Kuybyshev reservoirs, found that the carp louse *Argulus*, which sometimes infects other fishes, is particularly deadly to the zander; four to eight lice will kill a year-old zander in six hours, while carp and bream, the other possible hosts, are far more resistant. It may not be impossible to devise a sort of piscine myxomatosis to keep zander down. This may seem far-fetched, and indeed Gintort regarded the zander's susceptibility as bad news; but then the Russian zander catch runs into thousands of tons a year.

And this brings me to the last consolation; zander are really excellent food. I confess I am prejudiced in their favour; but then the first time I met zander was at Epernay in Champagne, in a fish pie, along with several of the sparkling local wines. It was a memorable meal; but they would not give me the recipe.

The Biter and the Leaper

To deceive a trout into biting a hook has been the great ambition and delight of a minority of men for a very long time indeed. The name "trout" by itself carries us back into the prehistory of angling, the most conservative of sports. Many European freshwater fish have names that have changed very slowly, and can be traced back to very primitive origins in the ancestral Indo-European language: unike the names of domestic animals, which vary rapidly and inexplicably from one time and place to another (horse, *cheval*, *Pferd*, *equus*. . .). The word "trout" goes back to an ancient root which was something like *trauz*, meaning to bite; the trout was The Biter to our Neolithic ancestors, as the bream was The Shiner. The salmon was The Leaper, too, but that is a more recent name, restricted to Western Europe. Further East its older name is preserved, as in the Yiddish *lox*; a name related to the Hindi *lakh*, a hundred thousand. In the crowded rivers of primaeval Europe, the migrating salmon were The Multitude.

These may have been no more than safe and convenient ways of referring to these fish, rather than their real ancestral names: there is a magic in names (omen, nomen, numen) and anyone who knows of the seventy-seven ways in which mediaeval English could avoid direct mention of "the deer that no man dare name", the hare, can easily suppose that men had some quite different real name for the trout when they were so interested in its biting habits in the neolithic age.

Hooks are even older than that; and the gorge was before the hook. Large hooks of stone and bone have survived from the early stone age – the oldest yet found are from Czechoslovakia, perhaps surprisingly – but they were made for bigger game than trout. Though even then, the hunters who lived in the caves of southern France during the last ice age made pictures of salmon, or perhaps sea-trout, carved on reindeer horn. But the first fly-fishers left no material remains; wooden rods and hair lines do not last, nor do small hooks even if they are made of materials more durable than the thorns and sharpened twigs that were the only choice before metals were known. (The same word means both "thorn" and "hook" in Latin; similarly in Hebrew). Even early modern fishing gear is extremely rare.

Words will often outlast the objects they describe. Written records of early fishing are of course very sparse; books that survive the centuries must have great good fortune, or literary virtues, or theological correctness; and most angling texts can rely only on the first. The classical writers at first mention fishing only incidentally. The Greeks regarded hauling on nets as deplorable labour, little better than slavery:

A mature cock-salmon fighting his way back upstream to breed. An exceptional feat of strength, agility and endurance nor did they appreciate angling, which Plato called a lazy, deceitful occupation, unworthy of a gentleman who would do better to take healthy exercise with horse and hounds. (One can only guess what he would have said of the modern Greek dynamite fishers.) But in Roman times morality softened; angling was then perceived to be a suitable occupation for a free man, since it encourages contemplation and requires much leisure and forethought. The poems of Martial, preserved through nineteen hundred years for their epigrammatic perfection and startling obscenity, include a debatable reference to fish being misled by flies; not a new invention even then, for the oldest record of flyfishing is perhaps a tomb painting from Egyptian Thebes. There, about 1500BC, an angler was depicted with a large winged insect beside his rod, though the detail is too poor to show if it was meant as bait or as an inevitable nuisance.

But the first clear description of the angler's art is in the writing of the mellifluous Aelian, who flourished around 200AD. He was an accomplished user of natural flies; his description of his delight in converting a buzzing, plaguing mosquito into successful bait for grayling proves that he had dextrous fingers and very fine hooks, or as vivid an imagination as any of his successors. He also mentions artificial flies as being essential for the rivers of Macedonia. There the fish will sometimes rise to one kind of fly, which loses its lustre and colour when dead. Therefore the Macedonian anglers took small hooks, and a twist of wool dyed crimson for the body, and some wax-red cock's hackles . . . and produced the original ancestor of the Red Spinner.

Aelian's works were valued for their fluent diversity rather than for their powers of logical exposition. It is never clear whether he meant to credit the Macedonians with the momentous discovery of the artificial fly, or only to stress its necessity in their waters. As he elsewhere mentions blue and red dyed wools, and feathers of various colours, as part of any angler's basic kit, he did not think of artificial flies as being peculiarly Macedonian in his own time. And though we now think of fly fishing as being predominantly for trout or salmon, Aelian does not say what exactly the Macedonians were after: "fish with speckled skins, but what the natives call them you had better ask in Macedonia," he says. The speckled skins sound like trout, and they (but not salmon, whatever Captain Fluellen may have said) are found in Macedonian waters; but classical writers were much happier with Mediterranean seafish than with the vaguely-known freshwater species of the savage north.

Just before the end of the Roman world, trout found their first definite literary mention in Ausonius' long and loving description of the Moselle. Then came the immigrating barbarians and universal darkness, in which all intelligible accounts of fishing disappear until the detailed pages, doubtless drawing on a continuous tradition, of the *Boke of St Albans*. One of the cherished legends of angling history attributes this account of field sports to Dame Juliana Berners, Prioress (or even Abbess) of Sopwell; for whose real existence there is no evidence except the name "Julians Bernes", mentioned once in the volume, ambiguously; but let us stay content with the legend and admire the book. Here, in the late fifteenth century, we find a dozen types of artificial fly, eleven of which had recognisable progeny in modern times: Olive, Yellow and Little Yellow May Duns; Wasp, Alder, Shell and Stone flies; Red Spinner, February Red and brown and light dressings of the Mayfly, to call them by their nearest modern names. Dame Juliana had a surprising knowledge, for a devout nun, of some points of angling – she gives a design for a collapsible rod which when folded looks like a walking stick, so that its user can go off for a stroll without arousing suspicion. Salmon she regarded as Big Game, "the most stately fish that any man may angle in fresh water"; rather beyond her usual tackle (she recommends a fifteen-strand line) but excellent food, always well appreciated by ecclesiastics. (It is no accident that twenty-five of the twenty-seven mediaeval English bishoprics lie on salmon rivers.) She also had a great appreciation of the trout, which she calls "a right deyntous fyssh and also a right fervente byter"; an unconscious echo of her Indo-European ancestors of six thousand years earlier.

Even such a gulf of time is very little in the history of fish. The salmonid family, to which all trout and salmon belong, have been recognisable for about sixty million years, since the close of the age of reptiles; they are most notably characterised by bearing two fins on their backs, of which the second, adipose (or flabby) fin has no rays and is much smaller and weaker than the first dorsal fin. The purpose of this weak fin is obscure; it is much larger, in proportion to the other fins, in the newly-hatched young and in the small parr; it may have some importance in the swimming of such small fish, though not in the adults.

Salmonids have not changed much from the primitive teleost stock, compared to more recent arrivals like the cyprinids. They are naturally abundant throughout the northern hemisphere; a few breed in the sea, but most need freshwater breeding-grounds with clear, well-oxygenated water and gravelly bottoms in which the females can scoop out redds to lay their eggs in, and in which the fry can hide. As adults they are less choosy; they commonly move downstream from the breeding ground, sometimes into lakes or out to sea, but they will need a generous supply of oxygen, and prefer cold tumbling streams where it dissolves well; or in placid waters they rely on what is dissolved in the rain or produced by waterweeds. (Hence the dilemma of the water-bailiff of a trout river in a hot, dry summer: cut too much weed and the trout will die or move elsewhere, cut too little and the anglers will catch no fish.)

All European trout, sea or (freshwater) brown trout, form one species, *Salmo trutta*, most closely related to the European salmon, *Salmo salar*; a trout is really a kind of small salmon that has the option of spending all its life in fresh water, instead of leaving for the sea after spending a year or more as a young freshwater parr. In a few places, even salmon have stopped migrating; there are dwarf, exclusively freshwater forms in the lakes of Norway, and in Lake Ohrid on the Albanian border (where they train bears to cure backache: the patient lies on his belly and the bear walks up and down his spine).

The young of salmon and of trout are remarkably similar, with a series of finger-print-like "parr marks" running down the body; even the adults are often confused. Liberal-minded magistrates in Scotland, where unlicenced unauthorised trout fishing can be legal when salmon fishing is not, have refused to convict on the grounds that small salmon cannot be infallibly distinguished from large sea trout. Actually there are small but invariable differences in the proportions of the mouth: the upper jaw runs back to below the rear edge of the eyeball in trout, only to the rear edge of the pupil in salmon; but anyone can make a mistake. Several of the old "record sea trout" have turned out to be salmon.

The native range of European trout stretches westward from the tributaries of the Aral Sea (once the easternmost arm of the Mediterranean) to the eastern Atlantic, and southwards from the White Sea to the northern Mediterranean, with an outlying population in the high Atlas. European salmon, that depend on the cold Greenland seas for

their adult food, do not breed so far south, but their far-ranging travels have taken them to both sides of the Atlantic.

Over most of their range, the culinary and sporting properties of salmon and trout are well appreciated; though not always. The Caledonians in the second century AD, says Dio Cassius, believed that each loch and burn had its resident nymph or goddess to whom the contents belonged, so they left the teeming fish untouched. (They have since found a better religion.) And in Eastern parts, as in ancient Greece, fishing is not sport but a labour. Witness the British Consul in Teheran who, in the brief happy period when such things were possible for an infidel and a diplomat, took a holiday by the Persian trout streams that flow into the Caspian. On the first day he caught a few fish; on the morning of the second the local dignitaries came to him with a great pile of shining tribute. Observing his great effort and small reward, they had caused their people to drag all the rivers with nets, overnight, for many miles . . . .

Trout vary considerably in different parts of their range, in size, markings and details of shape, far more than salmon do. Local patriotism once led to the recognition of ten different supposed species within the British Isles, some restricted to very small areas. Loch Leven alone claimed its own *Salmo Levenensis*, silvery trout with no red spots, of good flavour and fine sporting qualities, remarkable anatomically for the great number of finger-like protrusions from their intestines. So highly esteemed were Loch Leven trout that a special Act of Parliament was passed to make them the exclusive property of one local landowner, contrary to normal Scots law and natural justice. But by cross-breeding and transplanting different stocks it has been proved that all these "species" are only local races, and the differences between them are not hereditary but are produced by the different waters they live in. (Whether any Scots around Loch Leven drink the water, and if so what their intestines are like, I cannot say.)

Even a sea trout is only a brown trout that has chosen a bigger, more briny pond; and the choice can easily be altered. During the great colonial expansion of the last century, would-be anglers found themselves contemplating ideal trout waters in distant troutless countries; and by heroic efforts, with hundreds of thousands of best Itchen or Loch Leven eggs or fry kept cool by tons of ice, they succeeded in shipping trout to every southern continent. There the trout flourished mightily – occasionally killing off local species of fish, unmourned at the time, and at present imperilling the New Zealand ducks – and where the seas around were suitable, as in the Falkland Islands, some river trout rapidly became sea trout. Conversely, the freshwater trout of the Orkneys and Shetlands, and Iceland, must be sea trout that have abandoned the sea that alone could have brought them to those islands after the last ice age. And sea trout transported to reservoirs have offspring that after the second generation show no desire to return to the seas.

Similarly, the "ferox trout" of the older naturalists, inhabitants of

This six-pound rainbow trout patrolled the margin of the water for over twenty minutes, refusing everything offered. A vicious circle: catch one and you know what they are taking, but until you know what they are taking you won't catch one

big freshwater lakes that disdain flies but can be taken with minnows, are just big, old, lucky brown trout. The biggest are those of the southern Alpine Lakes; in Lake Como, said Paolo Giovio, a sixteenth-century Italian, they frequently reached a hundred pounds. In proportion to more mundane trout these would have been five feet long; believe him if you can. (In Loch Quoich they do really reach twenty pounds.) Pliny the younger, in Roman times, had a villa by Lake Como, built out on a pier so that he could cast a line from his bedroom, almost from in his bed. There's luxury for you.

American trout, though, are truly different from European. The beautiful rainbow trout, *Salmo gairdneri*, originally lived in the rivers of the Californian coast, the best coming from the tributaries of the Sacramento River. Its rapid growth, and higher tolerance of heat and turbid water, have made it a favourite in fish farms, and it is locally acclimatised in some English rivers.

All the salmon family are built for moderately fast cruising and for sudden dashes at nearby prey, not for speed over long distance. They have good streamlining and powerful muscles; but they have large, rounded fins that produce great thrust with a few strong strokes from a standing start, but which create too much drag to be suitable for very fast, prolonged chases. Those fish which are built for sustained high speed rather than for acceleration, mackerel or tuna for example, use more rapid strokes of much smaller, slenderer, more pointed fins that produce less thrust at low speed but less drag at high speed. (There is the same difference in shape between the wings of hawks and of falcons, for the same reasons.)

The trout, being a rather primitive teleost, has kept its paired fins in the original positions: fairly low on the body, with the pectoral fins well in front of the pelvic fins. Young trout still rest on the bottom, propped up on their pelvic fins.

The trout's swimming stroke has been studied more intensively than that of any other fish, partly because they breed well in captivity. Trout are the fish physiologist's equivalent of the laboratory rat, and the control group taste much better.

Slow-motion films of rainbow trout, startled by mild electric shocks or by balls dropped into the tank, show that they have two methods of lunging forwards. In one, the body is bent into an L- or C-shape and then straightened vigorously; in the other, the trout first forms an S-shape. In the first manoeuvre, the trout rapidly accelerates and simultaneously turns in the opposite direction to the C; but starting from an S-shape, the thrust is balanced so the trout moves straight forwards. Just before the lunge is made, the trout spreads its tail and unpaired fins so as to bring the greatest possible area into action; as the fish dashes forwards it lowers its fins so as to reduce their drag after the power stroke has been made.

Salmon, too, bend themselves into a C-shape before making their great leaps; Giraldus Cambrensis watched them springing up the falls of the Teifi, eight centuries ago:

A salmon bending itself into a C-shape

When they come to a seemingly impassable obstacle, they bend their tails round to their mouths. Sometimes, so as to leap with more force, they even put their tails into their mouths. Then with a great snap, as when a bough that has been held bent is loosed and straightens itself, they flick themselves out of this circular posture and leap up from the lower pool to the higher one, an astonishing sight to see.

Giraldus is not always reliable, and modern observation has not confirmed that salmon bite their tails, nor have physiological studies suggested that this could help them leaping. But to find out how the many surfaces contribute to the forward movement, physiologists still use the crude but effective method of amputating various fins and then seeing how the trout perform. The hydrodynamics of fish movement are so complex that theoretical calculations of the effects of different fins are quite impossible. (The movement of land animals is much more amenable to mathematics; dedicated physiologists have calculated that a cheetah with all four legs removed could still move at twenty miles per hour just by humping and straightening its elastic back, and the experimental test has not had to be performed.) It turns out that trout with all three vertical unpaired fins removed can still dash forwards as fast as ever, but lose control as they do so, yawing and rolling considerably. Removing the tail fins, though, does reduce the forward acceleration. It seems that the vertical fins are only stabilisers, and are too far forward to contribute much to the thrust, which is provided by the rear of the body and by the tail fins. But removing the tail fins of trout does not much affect their cruising speed; once trout are moving fast the extra area of the tail fins produces as much drag as thrust.

Young trout, for some reason, cannot perform S-shaped starts, and so can only take prey directly in front of them by following the first C-shaped stroke with later manoeuvres with opposite curvature that correct their turn but slow them down. To reverse the direction of turning completely after a C-shaped start is impossible without stopping altogether. But after an S-start a large trout can go rapidly ahead or alter course in either direction. So large trout can make more effective attacking manoeuvres than small trout. On the other hand, a small trout can go into a tighter turn from a C-start. A trout's turning circle has a minimum radius of one sixth of the fish's length; so a small trout can do a more effective escaping manoeuvre than a large one, which given the fish's cannibal propensities is as it should be.

The power of a trout's or salmon's forward rush is surprising; as is the skill with which an angler can control it. Large and small trout alike have been shown in laboratories to accelerate from a standing start, at their fastest, with a little over six times the force of gravity (six g, in colloquial physics). That is to say, a one-pound trout dashing forwards can pull with the force of a falling six-pound weight. Looked at another way, were it not for the resistance of the water from which it must start, a trout could just leap into the air carrying five times its own weight, which is more than I could, or you either I dare say. (But pike, that are better designed for forward lunges, can manage eight g.) Fortunately for anglers, if not for the makers of lines and reels, this acceleration can be maintained only briefly; for about seven hundredths of a second in the first forward stroke of a small trout, a tenth of a second for a large one. After the first powerful stroke, the swimming strokes are weaker because the fish would be slowed down if it bent its body into a very curved C- or S-shape. Even in a short sprint trout probably never exceed ten or twelve times their body length per second, according to scientists; and for big ones, less than this. In fact, there seems to be a general length-related speed limit for most fish, around ten body lengths per second; powerful fish like trout may manage a little better, sluggards like bream a little worse. There are exceptions; eels and similar slender fish

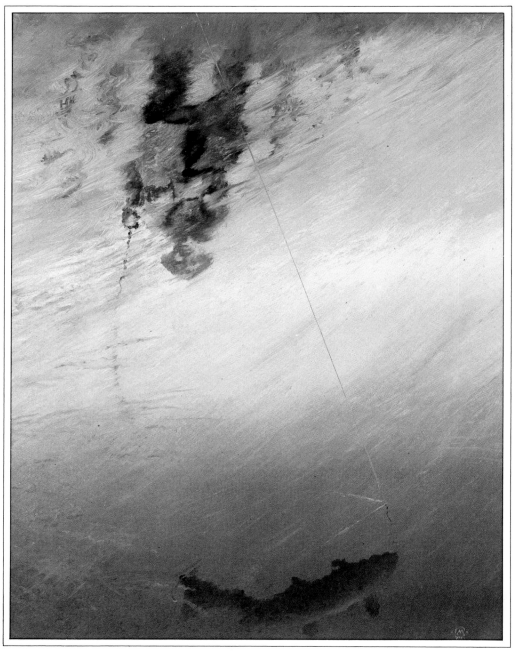

. . . sometimes golden wire
The glittering bellies of the Fly
* require;*
The Peacocks' Plumes thy
* tackle must not fail,*
Nor the dear purchase of the
* Sables' Tail.*
Each gaudy bird some slender
* tribute brings,*
And lends the growing Insect
* proper wings:*

that swim with slow, sinuous strokes can hardly manage two lengths a second; high-speed specialists like tuna have been reliably reported moving towards the horizon at over twenty. And big fish, and whales, are slower in proportion to their length; mercifully, for a blue whale swimming at ten body lengths per second (if such were possible) would be a hazard to shipping. Nevertheless, a big fish can always swim faster than a little fish; and, of two fishes of the same weight, a streamlined one like a trout will swim faster than a deep-bodied, manoeuverable one like a perch. A three-foot salmon can probably cruise at twelve feet per second.

Those anglers who would swear to at least double this even when sober must consider that scientists cannot get grants to go fishing and

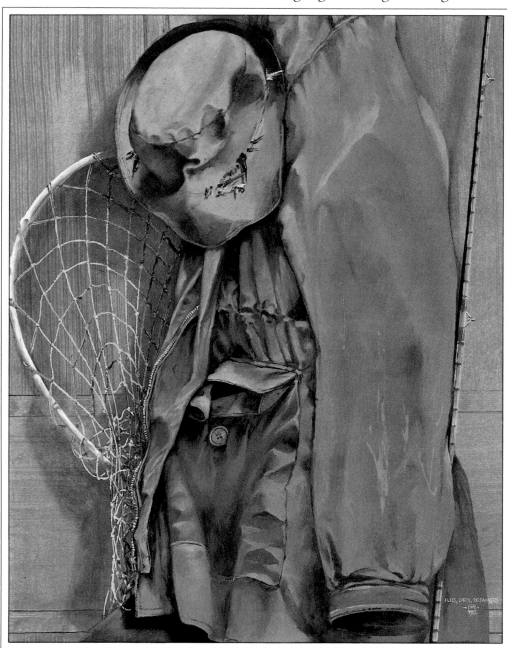

Silks of all colours must their aid impart,
And ev'ry Fur promote the Angler's Art.
So the gay Lady, with expensive care,
Borrows the pride of land, of sea, of air;
Furs, pearls and plumes the Painted Thing displays,
Dazzles our eyes, and easy hearts betrays.
(John Gay)

therefore base their estimates on laboratory trout that may not be trying their hardest. In principle one can calculate the speed of a hooked wild fish from the reading of a speedometer driven by the rotating reel, together with a simultaneous measurement of the angle the line makes with the water, ideally made by a friend standing to one side with a cine-camera. In practice this is likely to cause considerable argument.

These high accelerations and fast speeds of course only occur in the violent rushes of a fish escaping from danger or pursuing a prey it thinks likely to escape; which is why trout firmly impale themselves on plugs or spoons, which they take for some fast-moving target and dash at accordingly. Floating flies, which cannot move fast, usually seem worth much less effort to the trout, which may just sip at them and "drown them by pulling their hind legs underwater" after a lazy approach, unless some excitement drives them fast upwards. "The manner of the fishes taking flies, which is by rising to the surface of the water, and sometimes out of it, gives the Angler a very agreeable surprize," said old Bowlker, the eighteenth-century father of modern fly-dressing.

I heard of a man in Devon whose Jack Russell bitch, excited in her turn by leaping sea-trout, leapt overboard from the boat and caught the fish, or at least held its fins firmly enough to slow it down so it could be netted. Greatly encouraged, she progressed even to salmon. Unfortunately, her offspring do not share her habits.

Lacking such a marvellous beast, anglers must concentrate on deceiving the trout into thinking that a decorated hook is edible. Sometimes it is, partly. Trout will at various times try more or less any sort of meat: other fish, insects, worms, shrimps, snails, small mammals in time of flood, and in some rivers a floating waterweed that looks rather like a mollusc. The last two classes cannot be recommended as bait; though I am told by a usually reliable traveller that lemmings in Norway, in the seasons when they cast themselves into the fjords, are very serviceable. And in former times young mice before they had grown any hair, or red cherries in autumn, were much in favour.

But natural baits lack subtlety, even when cast with a catapult. Live baiting has had moments of grandeur, though not with trout; the seventeenth-century anglers who took great pike with a large live goose as bait should not be forgotten, nor imitated. And the tribes of Goodenough Island, off New Guinea, have the ultimate natural bait: an insect, zoologically classified as *Eurycanthra latro* (and what the natives call it you had better ask in New Guinea) which imitates a thorn twig to the extent of bearing sharp, curved thorns on its thighs and so acts as both bait and hook. A thread tied round the insect's leg completes the tackle. (This raises the considerable question, which I do not intend to answer, of how far fish mind being hooked in the mouth; presumably the New Guinea fish recognise the insect and could know it bears spikes.)

The deception is more skilful if the whole bait is artificial. Here there are two basic strategies. One is to create an imitation of the trout's natural food, either an exact copy of one particular item or something that generally suggests a possible prey, and rely on the trout's appetite to betray it. This is the older method, at least in theory: Aelian's Macedonians, and Dame Juliana Berners, had no doubt that their artifical flies were meant to imitate actual species. The other, more modern strategy is to make a very conspicuous object that resembles nothing on earth, and hope that the trout will be led by curiosity to see if the thing is edible. This strategy is modern in that it only came into conscious use with the lurid lures of recent times; but the older wet flies, which more or less conscientiously imitate winged adults that would not normally be found below the surface, are probably taken more through curiosity than from recognition, unless indeed they are mistaken for shrimps. (The tradition of abusing other people's choice of flies is a very old one; Charles Cotton himself was given a London-made trout fly and hung it in his parlour window to give his friends something to laugh at.)

Freshwater shrimp and imitation. Body of brown fur and lead wire. Bind on partridge hackle for ribs fore and aft. Cling-film strip laid on and bound with silver wire. Tease out fur with a comb

The unnatural approach is often rewarding, unless the trout have definite views about the day's menu. Trout that are feeding slowly are frequently indiscriminating, but if a large amount of one kind of food is available they concentrate on it. This is particularly the case when there is a hatch of waterflies. These spend most of their lives as underwater larvae, which trout will eat if they can catch them out of the cover of the bottom and the weeds; but when full grown and ready to metamorphose they rise to the surface as nymphs, hatch out into winged duns, disperse, breed and soon die. The period of hatching is peculiarly vulnerable, since the surface-bound insect is highly conspicuous and cannot move; and the flies use the same tactic as the wartime bomber streams over Germany. A multitude of defenceless targets, exposed to relatively few enemy, will lose far fewer of their number if they pass through the danger zone together, offering far more targets than the enemy can destroy in the time available, than if they spread their passage out over a long time. So flies synchronise their hatching; sometimes with wonderful results. In the summer of 1707, in London, they lay thick upon the pavements, on which footprints were visible as if after a fall of snow; and in the sunny August of 1973 so many mayflies were attracted by the hot surfaces of dark-painted cars in the Cambridgeshire villages around Shelford that they blistered the paint. The effects on trout are wonderful, too; when there is a hatch, the fish respond (either through force of habit or in frustration at not being able to bag them all) by concentrating their attacks on the hatching species, which must be identified by the angler and fairly well imitated by his fly. Sometimes, to complicate matters, the trout prefer the rising nymph to the hatching fly, or two or more species may hatch together, or spent adult flies from an earlier hatch may fall back into the water; and which the trout will favour cannot be predicted, but must be discovered.

Rainbow trout that were caught, sketched and eaten in less than two hours

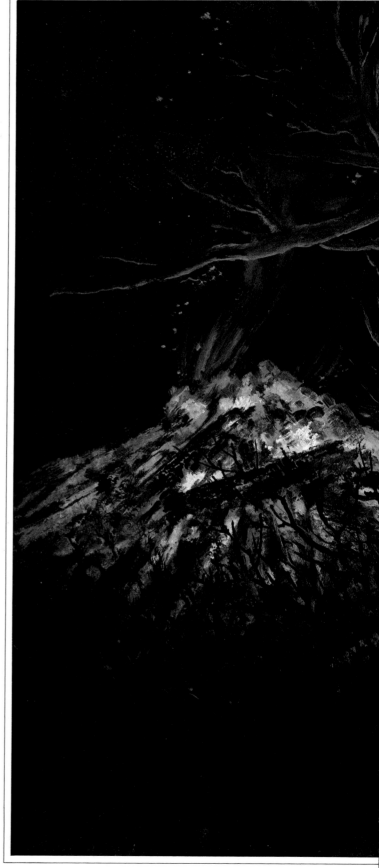

To create a convincing imitation, or to appeal to a trout's curiosity, we need to understand a trout's perception of its food. To judge by the size of the part of the brain that deals with vision, trout hunt largely by sight; but its view from underwater is different from a man's on land. The fish and the human eye both focus images through a lens onto a layer of light-sensitive rods and cones in the retina; but the trout's colour vision is red-biassed, though not so much as the perch's. And in human eyes the cones are packed densely into a small area at the back of the retina, and are relatively sparse elsewhere; in trout they are more evenly spread, though not perfectly uniform; the closest packing, in trout and most predatory fish, is in a band across the lower rear part of the retina, looking forwards and upwards. Even here the cones are only a fifth as closely packed as in the densest human area; so trout see as blurs what appear to us as fine patterns of colour.

And a trout's field of view is greatly different from a man's, and neglect of the differences has led some anglers into strange errors. Trout are often thought to be short-sighted, which they would be if they lived in air; and some people believe that since a trout's eyes are on the sides of its head it can see sideways but not in front. In proof of the latter it is argued that flies presented beside a trout will be taken, while in front they will be ignored. This mistaken belief would be true if a trout had a man's eyes. The differences are worth examining.

A human eye focusses light first through the curved surfaces of the eyeball, and then through the lens, lemon-shaped in cross section, that lies behind the iris. This works well in air; but underwater the eyeball surface nearly ceases to focus, for light passing from the water into the eye (which is optically very like water) is hardly bent at all. So a human eye becomes long-sighted when submerged. Also, the human eye concentrates on the view in front; very little of the retina deals with light coming from the sides, and acute vision at any instant is restricted to an arc of about five degrees, with the eyes continually moving to alter this field of detailed concentration.

Fish, by contrast, have the original fisheye lens, but more subtle than any camera's. They do not rely on focussing at the eyeball surface (which is nevertheless curved, so that fish out of water become short-sighted). A trout's lens is almost spherical, but built up of many concentric layers of different composition, so that the refractive index – the capacity of the material to bend light – is greatest in the centre. Such a lens, protuding through the iris instead of being behind it as in the human eye, can gather light over a field of 100 degrees and focus it uniformly across the retina with very little distortion. (If you look at a trout or any other sizeable fish swimming in a tank at an aquarium or restaurant, you will see what looks like a black or dark brown sphere in the middle of each eye, and from almost any angle you can see part of at least one of these spheres. In fact the spheres are transparent; what you are seeing is the retina through the lens, and wherever you can see the retina the fish can see you.) The disadvantage of this design is that the iris serves only to prevent light getting into the eye round the side of the lens; it cannot contract to protect the retina from bright light, since the lens protrudes so much through it. So trout near the surface on a bright day are easily dazzled by the sun. Not entirely, though, for instead of contracting the pupil they can withdraw the light-sensitive cells deeper into the retina, which gives some relief. In fact, fishes have a daily rhythm of movement of the cells in the retina; all other things being equal, the cones move to the upper layer of the retina in the day and go deep at night; the rods do the reverse. This daily rhythm must mean that a fish at midday does not see the same fly that it sees earlier or later in the day, even if the amount of light is similar.

Since the trout's lens has a very short focal length, changes in the distance of objects looked at make very little differences in the distance behind the lens at which the image is focussed. The retina is thick enough for the trout to have everything more than a yard away in focus simultaneously over most of its field of view. With this deep-field wide-angle vision, it hardly matters that the trout's eyes are nearly immobile; not so fixed, though, as an owl's eyes which cannot be moved in their sockets even with pliers. A trout's fields of vision actually overlap in front by about 30 degrees, and the only blind area is the 30 degrees rearwards; whereas in men the rear blind field covers nearly 160 degrees. Hence one of the advantages of casting upstream; the trout head into the current where drifting food comes from, and the angler can be in their blind field.

If trout do in fact prefer food appearing at their side, it is partly because they can set at it with a C-shaped start and partly because their lenses are not absolutely spherical. There is a flattening in front, so that when a trout's eyes are relaxed its forward view is short-sighted, with objects more than eight inches away out of focus. More distant objects can be brought into focus if the trout's interest is aroused, by pulling the lens closer to the retina; but if a trout is thinking about nothing in particular it will be looking with built-in bifocals at the space immediately in front of its nose, and also in the distance to its flank and rear. So distant casts will be more likely to meet with a response from an inactive trout if they are to one side. Hence also the safety of a downstream cast to busy rising fish whose forward vision is focussed on the nearby surface.

The scope of a trout's view is also much affected by the distortions due to reflection and refraction, or bending, of light at the surface between air and water. This is most important; the trout normally sees the angler in air from water, until it is too late. Also, trout like to see their targets against the light from above and will attack from below for choice, even if the prey is another fish swimming well below the surface. (This is partly because the colour-sensitive cones are packed more densely in the lower part of the retina, where light from above falls.) A fly at or near the surface, seen against or in the region, is therefore in the preferred target zone, as well as being where the angler can observe and control events instead of having to react to happenings in the deeps.

For centuries the technique of "angling aloft on the water", in the Tudor phrase, has been practised; the method used to obtain the

advantageous result has varied with the materials available. Before the mid-seventeenth-century invention of reels, all the strain of a pull had to be taken by the long rod and the fixed line; before silkworm gut became available (at first in Switzerland in the 1720s) the line had to be of hair; and though experts claimed that the largest trout that swims could be taken on a single hair, most anglers felt safer with nine or a dozen strands, fifteen or even thirty for a salmon. Even so, a common practice on hooking a really large fish was to throw line, rod and all into the river and hope that they could eventually be retrieved with the exhausted monster still attached.

With such a rope of a line there could be no question of a modern style of casting flies. The technique was to cast always down-wind, with a fly dressed to swim on or near the surface. (Cork foundations for bodies to make them buoyant were recommended as early as 1590.) A many-stranded hair line is thick but light for its width, so the wind would act powerfully to keep it aloft, and nearly all could be kept off the water while the fly floated or sank a little. The idea of keeping a dry fly drifting in the surface film, like the most vulnerable hatching or spent flies, came a few generations after the fine silk lines that made it possible, in the early nineteenth century. (The first definite mention of dry flies comes from Axminster in Devon, in 1852; though to Hampshire men it is a moral certainty that the invention was made earlier, and on the Test or Itchen.)

Both dry and wet flies, or the angler using either, are subject to the same optical effects. Light coming vertically down passes straight into still water; as the angle it makes with the surface decreases, it is to an increasing extent partly reflected and partly refracted downwards, till light striking the water almost horizontally is bent downwards to an angle of about 42 degrees to the surface. Any point underwater, therefore, is at the tip of an inverted cone of light coming from the entire field of view above the water. So when a trout looks up it sees a clear round disc, about twice as wide as the fish is deep, through which it can see out of the water from the horizon upwards in all directions. This is sometimes called Snell's window, after the physicist whose law explains it, and sometimes the fishes' window, after earlier observers. Beyond the edges of the window the water surface acts as a mirror, reflecting downwards any light from below; so that a trout sees some underwater things twice, once directly and once in the mirror.

It is a distorting window even when unwrinkled. Anything near the horizon appears at the edge of the window, dimmed because most of the light striking the water at a shallow angle is reflected, and seemingly compressed downwards and therefore more distant because of the great refraction. Also, very near the edge of the window different colours are refracted to perceptibly different extents, red least and violet most, so a multi-coloured object seems to split up into overlapping patches of different colours. At the extreme edge this effect is so great as to decompose images entirely; on a bright, very calm day the fishes' window is fringed with a complete rainbow, red innermost. Above this

Leopard trout seen from a footbridge

appear objects on land, looking very compressed and far away.

To give some examples of this apparent distancing: something reaching six feet above the surface, six feet away, fills an angle of 45 degrees, halfway from horizon to zenith, when seen from just above the surface. Seen from just below the surface, the tip of the same object seems only 16·5 degrees above the edge of the window, the same angle that it would make from twenty feet away seen only through air. (The width of the object, however, will not be affected, though it will be to some extent spread out round the edge of the window. All anglers seem remarkably fat to the trout.)

Further away, the compression rapidly increases. At five yards an object six feet above the surface, again seen from just below the surface, fills the angle above the edge of the window that it would at twenty-six yards if it were seen undistorted; at twenty yards, it has the apparent height it would have undistorted at a hundred yards; at fifteen, two hundred and fifty; at twenty, over five hundred. So a prudent angler fishing from a distance is a difficult sight for a trout to interpret and recognise. The difficulty can in one way be lessened if the fish goes deeper; a trout six feet down would see something ten yards away horizontally and six feet above the surface with the height it would have if undistorted at only fifty-eight yards, instead of a hundred; at fifteen, as if at a hundred and forty-eight; at twenty, two hundred and eighty. But though a wary trout lying deep has a better view of the shore than one feeding at the surface, it is a view more coloured by the water. Green clothing helps anglers to blend with this coloured foreground, even if there is nothing else green behind them.

Such camouflage may be taken too far; it was, by Dr Thomas Birch, who around 1750 "in order to deceive the fish ... had a dress constructed, which, when he put it on, made him appear like an old tree. His arms he conceived would appear like branches, and the line like a long spray. In this sylvan attire he used to take root by the side of a favourite stream, and imagined that his motions might seem to the fish to be the effect of the wind. He pursued this amusement for some years in the same habit, till he was ridiculed out of it by his friends." What else are friends for?

Even if you wade into the water, unless the trout is actually swimming round your ankles it can see no connection between the inoffensive submerged parts, which it can see directly until they disappear into the mirror (and which it may never have seen clearly through the window unless you stand on your head on the bank), and the rest of you seen far away through the window. I suspect that herons and storks also benefit from this optical illusion. Similarly, men in a boat must seem to a fish to be far above, and far beyond, the submerged parts of the hull.

When the water surface is disturbed, both mirror and window are distorted. In rough water, the window splits up into many transient patches, which give small warped pictures of the world above the water and are rapidly replaced by equally warped reflections of the world below; neither can be clearly interpreted, so a gust of wind may offer an angler a chance to move nearer to a wary trout, or to make a cast, without frightening it. Smaller ripples give local distortions of the window. A trout that stations itself in a quiet pool enjoys a better view, as well as a less strenuous effort to stay in place, than it would in more rapid water.

A leash of rainbow trout

Some hold that flies on or near the surface are only visible when they enter the window. Certainly they will then stand out dark against a light background; for which reason the importance of having a light–coloured, if not translucent, line has long been recognised. (Plutarch sensibly recommended hair from the tail of a white horse for the length next the bait; he added that stallion's or gelding's hair is preferable, since a mare's urine weakens the tail. Modern biochemistry has shown that urea does in fact destroy protein structure; whether the effect on a mare's tail is significant has not been tested.)

But there are other factors to consider. A nymph or wet fly near the surface, beyond the window seen by a trout, will be at the tip of the cone of light coming in through its own window. As this light hits the bristles and the transparent or glossy parts of the body, it will be scattered and reflected in all directions, including the direction of the trout; so it will be conspicuous though outside the window. And a dry fly floating outside the window will warp the surface so much that light will be seen coming in around it. This will again be conspicuous, especially if small iridescent air bubbles are trapped along with the fly.

The dimpled surface around a floating fly must also warp its apparent shape considerably; though if an artificial is a good imitation of a natural species, and sits on the water similarly, the warped images should be similar also. Possibly trout are so used to seeing things distorted in and through the surface that inconstancy of shape matters less to them than to us. This might explain why they sometimes ignore the dark unnatural barbed tail that curves under the otherwise lifelike artificial fly; a defect in imitation that can be avoided in dry flies by setting the hackles reversed, so that the hook is held above the surface; or, in the cunning USD flies of Mr John Goddard, reversing the hook: but not in a wet fly, till someone finds how to make it transparent. (Maybe something could be done with ultra-fine glass fibres in clear resin.) But this can only be speculation; though we can follow the path of light through air and

water, and even into the fish's eye, the refraction of the image through the trout's mind is beyond calculation.

Deceiving a trout with a fly is entirely a matter of deceiving its sight. It can to a certain extent detect movement in the water; but most flies, real or artificial, are too small to make any useful noise. No doubt the chaos in the water made by a spoon or plug, or a thrashing live bait, attracts trout; it can hardly much resemble the wake of a normal swimming fish, but that is all to the good, since an apparently crippled or frantic prey is likely to seem easy meat. Sophisticated electronic lures that emit a high-frequency buzz to imitate a mosquito's whine have been tried; unfortunately, trout cannot hear high-pitched noises. The ancient art of tickling, though, does depend on persuading the fish that the motions of your hand are those of weed or water; an invaluable gift, for those that can do it. Perhaps the greatest exponent of tickling was the Abbé de la Fai, the natural brother of the Duc d'Orléans, who accompanied him on a visit to England just before the Revolution. He claimed to be able to draw any fish out of the water, by tickling it with a little switch; and was about to demonstrate his art, at Newmarket, when the Prince of Wales took hold of his heels and tipped him into the pool. Royalty have their own sense of humour.

Sounds and splashes may nevertheless be used to attract trout. Among the fishermen of Reay in Sutherland in the last century, disappointing days of fishing from boats were enlivened by throwing one of the party overboard, and hauling him in "exactly as if he were a fish"; or so said the minister, the Rev. J. Macdonald. Perhaps "exactly" is an over-statement; if not, I hope the hook was blunt and the priest padded. Soon afterwards, we are told, the trout would start to bite.

Maybe this method would still work, but it seems a reversal of the normal order of nature for the angler to enter the water so thoroughly. The Victorians were more hardy than us; the advice never to wade in deeper than the fifth button of your waistcoat, and to examine your legs after entering frozen waters and return home if they are black or purple, was given in all seriousness. Nevertheless, such contrarieties are always possible, and memorable; the ultimate misfortune being that of one Parmis, son of Callignotus, whose epitaph from the third century BC tells us that he held a fine fish in his mouth while changing his lure, and its dying convulsions carried it down into his throat.

Angling provokes the most unlikely moralists to revel in such disasters, real or imagined: Byron wished that Izaac Walton might have been hooked by a trout, and Peter Pindar, satirist of George III and his times, provides a verse appropriate for ending this attempt at a trout's-eye view:

> *Enjoy thy stream, O harmless Fish;*
> *And when an Angler, for his dish*
> *Through gluttony's vile sin,*
> *Attempts, the wretch, to pull thee out*
> *God give thee strength, O gentle Trout,*
> *To pull the Raskal in!*

Yorkshire trout stream. Not the gin-clear chalk streams of the south but turbulent, wet-fly water

It would be extreme misfortune to be pulled in by a normal trout; big salmon are another matter. Eight feet is not an impossible leap for a salmon, and it can have a great deal of weight to throw about. Sixty-four pounds is the recognised British rod-caught record, achieved in 1922 by Miss G. W. Ballantyne (to whom I apologise for writing of anglers as if they were all males). But salmon have come bigger; the eighth Earl of Hume took one of sixty-nine pounds twelve ounces from the Tweed in the 1730s; the Bishop of Bristol lost a seventy-one pounder in 1871, when his trace broke after ten and a half hours of struggle, but recognised the fish when it was netted the next day, further down the Tay. An eighty-two pounder was netted in the same river in 1869. And over in America, the chinook salmon (that will swim over two thousand miles up the Yukon to its spawning grounds) has been netted at one hundred and twenty-six pounds, and caught on a rod, heroically, at ninety-two.

The Pacific chinook has not been brought to European waters; the humpback, *Oncorynchus gorbuscha*, has been brought by the Russians to

A five-pound humpback cock salmon lunging for a spinner. Spectacular sport; extraordinary breeding colour

the White Sea and is occasionally reported in the Shetlands and off northern Scotland. It has the most spectacular breeding livery, and deformations, of any salmonid, but does not excel in size.

Such successful transplantation (and the similar establishment of Atlantic salmon in the southern oceans) is relevant to one of the great mysteries of the salmon; their navigation across a thousand miles of sea, or more, from their feeding grounds to spawn in the streams they were born in. Transplanted salmon fry return, not to their place of birth, but to the waters they grew up in. This makes the stocking of salmonless rivers possible; but the accurate return of specimens marked when young has puzzled biologists for years. It seems, now, that the salmon rely on several methods to get home, and do not always navigate correctly; fortunately for the species, since fish that infallibly return to the river of their birth would never be able to colonise new territories when the climate changes.

In open waters, salmon steer partly by the sun and partly by the earth's magnetic field. Like most vertebrates, they have a small iron-rich region in their head which allows them to sense the direction of magnetic north. In Canadian experiments, salmon diverted into a large, circular tank surrounded by an electromagnet swam across the tank on the correct magnetic bearing when the magnet was off, and were diverted when the magnetic field was altered; but they could only be deceived when the sky was obscured. In fact, celestial navigation is in the long run more reliable than magnetic; for every thirty thousand years, or thereabouts, the earth's magnetic field dies down and then re-establishes itself with the poles reversed, which would bring disaster to anything steering by magnetic north alone. The last such magnetic reversal was around forty thousand years ago; let us be grateful for the invention of the gyrocompass.

This magnetic sense is not used by most humans; but we too have a zone rich in magnetised crystals, in our nasal sinuses; and experiments in Manchester have shown that blindfolded, disoriented students can feel which way is north unless they are distracted by magnets. (For some reason women do better than men.)

Even though such navigation may bring salmon back to the same coastal region they set out from, it does not explain how they choose the right river, and even the right stream, of so many. This seeems to be largely a matter of smell; artificially flavouring the water, and then a few years later switching the flavour to a nearby stream, makes salmon home

Fresh-run salmon

on the flavour, not the place. It may seem odd to speak of the sense of smell in a fish; some imagine that as we taste water and smell the air, so fish can only taste their surroundings; but it is not so. Fish need to distinguish between the flavour in their mouth of whatever they are sampling, and the flavour in the water they swim in; they take a steady flow of water into their nostrils, from which olfactory nerves run to the brain, quite separate from the nerves that supply the taste-buds in the mouth. And that it is smell, not taste, that leads migrating salmon home can be shown by stopping their nostrils after they arrive at the estuary; unable to smell out their way, they blunder confusedly.

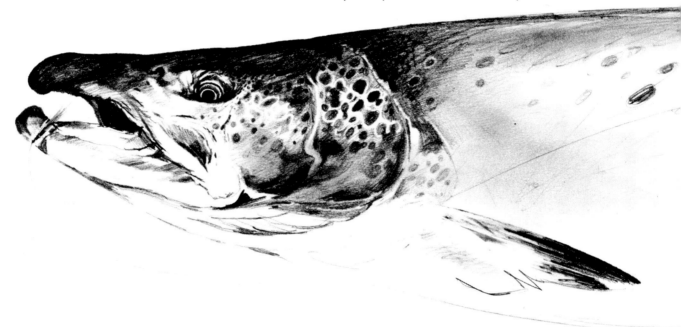

The salmon has a head worthy of the king of game fish: and the Hapsburg jaw

The late Mr Eric Linklater had a morbid fancy that what attracts salmon upstream may be the scent of the decomposing carcasses of the fish that bred earlier, and did not recover from the effort of spawning; a baseless supposition, for salmon transplanted as fry return to waters in which no salmon has bred, or died, for generations. This has recently been achieved even in the Thames, where in the summer of 1982 over twenty fish were found ascending Molesley weir, survivors of those released some years earlier in the repurified river.

The other great mystery of the salmon is the highly practical one of why they can be caught by angling at all. Migrating fishes often fast; salmon seem not to eat at all after they enter fresh water. At any rate, the stomachs of those taken are invariably empty, and over prolonged ascents they lose much weight. This is in a way merciful; the great multitudes of migrating salmon that were common before commercial fishing and pollution would have devoured most of the freshwater life in their path, had they paused to eat. (A Russian geologist prospecting in Siberia described one of the remaining multitudinous salmon-runs in awestruck terms, "as if a second river, greater than the first, was flowing uphill". Such was the Thames, once.)

Nevertheless, migrating salmon are taken with flies or baits which they attack as if they were trout feeding. Not, of course, with the caution of an experienced brown trout, for they have no adult freshwater experience; without the demanding taste in imitations. The larger and more lurid the salmon-fly, the better; "gaudy and orient," said General Venables of the successful salmon-flies even of the seventeenth century. Some suppose that salmon take flies out of irritation, or aggressiveness, rather than as food. And yet, as those who cannot afford the expensive art of fly-fishing know well, salmon will eagerly take a slowly-drifting bunch of worms or a swiftly darted, lifelike shrimp; surely they must recognise these as some sort of food?

Is it not possible that salmon taste the food of the rivers they ascend, as well as smelling the water, to see if their palate is reminded of the species they preyed on when they were young parr? An educated taste can distinguish between Speyside malts, or different vintages; may not the fauna of a particular stream have its own bouquet which has only to be sampled to be recognised, and then spat out in the best tasting fashion? Perhaps salmon home by smell and taste alike, and are perturbed if either is amiss; and in the experiments with strong artificial flavours, these may have been so strong as to overwhelm all other sensations.

The flavour of salmon themselves needs no recommendation. "Any fool can see that the Lake District is beautiful, but it takes a real artist to appreciate the Fens" is a consoling proverb in East Anglia; similarly, the test of a fish-cook's skill is to make a tench or bream delicious. The colouring of the flesh may contribute to the appeal; it is derived from the pigments of the marine shrimps on which the salmon feed, and is hard to imitate in farmed salmon without dyestuffs. (Flamingoes, likewise, are coloured pink because of their diet, and bleach in captivity; the theory that they are coloured for camouflage, being invisible as they fly home in the evenings against the lurid African sunsets, has only ingenuity to recommend it.) I have heard the lament that there are no longer smoked salmon like the old red fish of Gloucestershire, that were preserved over a fire of mingled oak-dust and dried horse-dung; the commercial article is good enough.

While it lasts. Commercial netting off the estuaries, and in the Greenland feeding grounds, has gone far to destroying the former multitudes. In King Edward II's time the polar bear in the Tower of London was set loose on a rope, to catch its supper from the salmon ascending the Thames; all the restocking and purification in the world will not provide such sights again.

Ice-age Relics

An angler who has just discovered the sport is commonly so excited to find that catchable fish lurk beneath the surface of his local water, and so occupied in raising a few of them above it, that he does not stop to wonder why those particular fish inhabit that particular reach. If he angles in man-made still waters, indeed, the question is often soon answered: the Committee of the Angling Club had them put there. In other places, the distribution of fishes is governed by factors no less arbitrary and unquestionable; the nature of the water and the chances of history.

No two rivers or lakes are alike, and a philosopher would say, no-one fishes twice in the same river. But an experienced angler can view any stretch of water in the country and estimate the species that ought to be found there. And when he is wrong it will usually be because chance has prevented a species that would flourish in that place from reaching it. The factors to be considered in estimating the likely inhabitants are the speed of flow of the water, its temperature, the amount of sediment and vegetation in it, and in consequence of these the probable oxygen content; and all are interconnected; and all are very different now from what they were only fifteen or twenty thousand years ago, at the climax of the last ice age. Early men already practised angling of a sort in Europe then, and there were a few rare wanderers in frozen Britain; at Pavilland in Gower they buried their dead in a cave only a few miles south of the edge of the glaciers. They would have found most of our modern fish absent, and the streams below the glaciers stocked with species that now hide in the hill streams and in mountain lakes. The charr and the whitefish - powan, pollan and vendace - are Arctic species that have certainly been here since the last glaciation; the grayling, too, is a cold-loving fish that has been driven from the lowland waters that are now warm and still. All these fish, and to a lesser extent the trout and salmon, are restricted by their breeding habits (for they cannot breed in warm water and need mud-free bottoms to spawn on) and by their need for oxygen which is most abundant in cold water. The coarse fishes, mostly newcomers by comparison, are summer breeders, can make do with less oxygen and generally prefer mud. Consequently they abound in the modern lowlands, except where geographical barriers have stopped them spreading north after the cold retreated; their occasional absence, then, is a sort of negative relic of the last ice age. The positive relics are hiding in hill streams and deep lakes, waiting for the cold to return and drive back the newcomers; with five or ten thousand years to wait, on past form, perhaps less.

For we are well past the warmest part of the present interglacial interlude; to judge from the traces of past interglacials, we can expect our climate to become steadily colder, though slowly. No-one can say

Coregonid whitefish in a lakeland winter, the only season it can leave the cold deeps

for certain what forces drive the alternating cycles of glacial and interglacial periods, but the course of their progress is tolerably clear.

There have been at least seven cold and seven warm periods during the present batch of ice ages, which between them have covered perhaps two million years. The warm interglacials are relatively short, around twenty thousand years each; the last one was warmer than the present has ever been, for tropical beetles then left their remains in the Thames gravels, and together with the more usual beasts of Europe the hippopotamuses wandered far north. Their unmistakable teeth have been found even in Stockton-on-Tees, as far from the tropics as Tierra del Fuego or the southern arm of Hudson's Bay. Not that Britain was then tropical; a little more moderation of the winters, perhaps only raising the average temperature by 2°C, would allow hippopotamuses to survive here now.

But as interglacials end the temperature drops in all the northern lands, and a much longer cold period begins. The warmth of the last interglacial ended around ninety thousand years ago; our trees gave place to conifers and birches, then to the shrubs and grasses of the modern Arctic tundra.

This tundra could not have been quite like anything on earth today; the fossil vegetation would suit a climate with an average temperature about 8°C below today's values, but modern tundras are found only in the far north where the summer sun cannot rise high in the sky. Early glacial Britain may have had long, bleak, tree-killing winters with quite warm midsummers. The river deposits at Brandon in Warwickshire, from this period, were laid down when no trees grew apart from the dwarf willows that survive by the fringes of Siberian rivers today; but summer-breeding pike, gudgeon, minnows, chub, roach and perch still swam in the streams.

The deepest cold, and the most widespread glaciation, was reached just before the whole process went mysteriously into reverse, shortly before the start of the present interglacial. At the height of the last glaciation, about eighteen thousand years ago, the British ice-cap lay five thousand feet deep or more over its centre in the Scottish Highlands. The southern limits of the ice can be traced from the Wash, along the east coast, lapping round the Yorkshire moors, covering the Pennines and the Cheshire plain, spreading erratically across the western Midlands and over all but the extreme south of Wales.

As the last interglacial was warmer than this, so the last glacial was less extensive than its predecessors. Earlier ice-sheets had covered East Anglia and the Midlands, south up to the Cotswolds and the Chilterns, with a disastrous effect on the landscape. The rounded, rolling hills and steep water-cut escarpments of southern England have never known the ice; the hard rocks of Wales and the North have been sculpted into deep valleys by the small glaciers of the first and final stages of each ice-age, and preserved beneath a deep immoveable cover through the worst periods; but the softer earths that lie between have been scraped and planed by a broad, fast-moving mass of ice, and pushed into a shapeless jumble of flattened mud: good coarse fishing country, though.

Nowadays, that is; but not when the rivers around the glaciers were frozen for most of the year and, in their summer spate, carried enormous volumes of meltwater, whose rapid flow laid down the great gravel beds in what are now the valleys of slow, winding, silt-laden rivers. Only cold-loving species that breed on mud-free bottoms could have flourished around the ice; among them, certainly, the Arctic charr, *Salvelinus alpinus*, which of all present British fish is the most adapted to extreme cold. It flourishes further north than any other freshwater species; charr are to be found even in the summer streams of glacial meltwater in the north of Greenland and Ellesmere Island, and if there were land nearer the Pole they would doubtless swim there too. The Arctic forms have lives like salmon, feeding as adults in the sea but entering fresh running water to breed. In the last ice age charr likewise swam from the cold seas up the glacier-fed rivers of Europe; as the ice melted, some charr followed the cold northwards, others clung to their old spawning grounds around the diminishing glaciers. Eventually some of the southern populations could no longer pass downstream to the sea, as the lowland rivers had become unbreathably hot; just as an outlying population of trout are now trapped in the mountain streams of the high Atlas, cut off from the Mediterranean by the increasing heat of the coastal plains. Outlying populations of charr similarly survive in the lakes and ice-fed streams of the Alps (hence the *alpinus* in the name).

They also hide in the deep still waters of the French Cevennes, the English Lake District, Scotland, North Wales and the north of Ireland; here were glaciers ten thousand years ago, but no longer. The charr have moved upstream from their old spawning grounds, into the cold sanctuaries that the glaciers gouged out between the mountains, and filled when they melted. It is these deep lakes that have allowed Arctic fishes to survive the warmer modern climate; unlike Arctic land animals trapped in Britain as the ice receded. (The last of these, the reindeer that once roamed as far south as the Pyrenees, may have lingered in Sutherland till the twelfth century; Norse sagas speak of the earls of Orkney journeying to the north of Scotland to hunt them.) These concealed lake charr have mostly abandoned the flowing waters even for spawning, choosing instead the gravelly bottoms in the shallows of the lakes; except for the Windermere charr, some of which still ascend the Brathay, though not the neighbouring, slightly warmer Rothay.

Charr spawn in either autumn or spring; the same lake may have two different breeding stocks. They choose water at its densest, at 4°C. The breeding livery can be spectacular; dark back, silver-blue sides with reddish spots, and an astonishingly vivid red and orange belly. The colours are best seen in the migratory charr of the far North; the isolated lake fish are more sombre. They are red enough, though, to give the fish their name, from the Gaelic *ceara*, meaning red. (The Scots pronunciation is more accurately charrrr.) The southern lake charr are diminished in size, too; two pounds is the British record, while Canadian specimens have been taken up to twenty-seven pounds. The closely related *Salvelinus namaycush*, a more southern species in America, grows to one hundred and two pounds; a freak specimen, admittedly, one netted in Lake Athabasca that had failed to mature sexually and so had put into bone and flesh what others spend in spawn.

Any method of angling that will take trout will also take charr, if they will come close enough to the surface; the shoals of Arctic charr in the deep lakes often stay hidden. An introduced charr, the American brook "trout", *Salvelinus fontinalis*, has established itself in a few lochs and streams and is more of a surface feeder. Again, it can be taken, and cooked, as if it were a trout. It has a distinctive appearance; like all charr, it has light spots on a dark background rather than the reverse pattern seen in trout and salmon (the other distinguishing mark is that the teeth in a charr's mouth do not extend down the vomer, the bone in the middle of the upper palate.) In the brook charr, the back is a darkish green, and the paler spots are drawn out to form an intricate pattern of wriggles and blobs; excellent camouflage in dappled light.

The other glacial survivors among British fish are the whitefish of the genus *Coregonus*; closely related to the salmonids, with the same characteristic adipose dorsal fin, but now placed in a separate family. They have larger scales than the salmonids, a uniform silvery colour and generally a weak mouth with small teeth. The coregonids are a taxonomist's nightmare, for though they will inhabit cold rivers and brackish waters they prefer deep cold lakes, where they have formed isolated local populations which differ from one lake to another and may or may not be different species. The prevailing view at present is that the whitefish of the British lakes comprise two species only, *Coregonus albula* and *C. lavaretus*. (Another species, *C. oxyrinchus*, the houting, with a prominent pointed snout, has occasionally come up rivers from the North Sea.) *C. albula* is found in some Irish loughs (Neagh, Erne, Derg and Ree), where it is called the pollan; also in Derwentwater, and in Bassenthwaite Lake further down the Derwent, and in the Scottish lochs near Maben. In these lakes it is known as the vendace – a name that is one of the rare survivals of the old Gaulish language, in which *vindos* meant white. It is distinguished by its projecting lower jaw from *C. lavaretus*, which is known as the powan in Loch Lomond and Loch Eck, as the skelly in Cumberland (in Haweswater, Ullswater and Red Tarn) and as the gwyniad in Llyn Tegid in Wales. Both also occur sporadically, growing bigger than the pound or two of British dwarfs, in lakes around the Baltic and in northern Russia, under a variety of names; though these complexities are as nothing to the problems that confront Canadian zoologists when they study their eighteen or more species of whitefish in their infinity of lakes.

In the French Alps, where the cold lakes also hold whitefish left over from the last glaciation, they serve them baked on a bed of mushrooms or shallots, with white wine and cream blended into the sauce.

Whitefish and charr hide in deep mountain lakes because these have cold, clear, oxygen-rich water, like that which once flowed in the glacier-fed rivers; other salmonids avoid lowland plains of heat and mud.

A lakeland brook charr of just over two pounds

Vendace, right, powan, top and sharp-nosed houting, all with upward-staring eyes

One cold-loving species, whose European distribution is obviously an ice-age relic, prefers flowing rivers to lakes; the grayling, *Thymallus thymallus*. This fish is something of an anomaly; related, obviously, to trout and salmon and whitefish, with the distinctive adipose fin, but with a very large sail-like first dorsal, in which the rearmost rays are much lengthened so that the rear edge trails even when the fin is erect. It is a purely freshwater fish, unlike the salmonids; but its greatest difference from the other game fish is in its breeding habits. Though it likes cold water – it and the charr are reckoned to be the only fish that feed better below 4°C than above – and must spawn on gravel, it breeds not in winter, but in the milder conditions of spring, from March to May. The female lays relatively many eggs, three to four thousand for each pound of her weight, four or five times as many as a trout of the same size; and the eggs are smaller, and the embryos develop quickly, more like a summer-breeding coarse fish. Grayling need water from 10–15°C to breed in; therefore, though their love of cold keeps them from spreading as far south as the trout, holding them in the Alps and Carpathians, and across the northern European plain to the White Sea and Scandinavia, they may also have kept their distance from the glaciers. In Continental rivers the "grayling zone" is downstream of the trout zone, in the cool fast-flowing but not barren region that in Britain is called the minnow zone. For grayling are patchily distributed across Britain; they seem to prefer, or at least only be prominent in, waters that are at least five yards across, and these are uncommon in hilly regions on this small island.

The preference for regions below the trout zone, where some weeds grow, is due to the grayling's feeding habits; it is more of a bottom feeder than trout, snapping up caddis larvae and midge pupae and the eggs of other fishes, including trout or salmon, where their habitats overlap, to the distress of water-bailiffs. In the southern trout streams, for this reason, grayling are ill regarded; in the lakes and rapid torrents of the north, they are better liked. For one thing, their eccentric breeding habits mean that they are in season when trout aren't; for another, angling for grayling has its own skills. Float-fished worms are more acceptable; I have heard that the big grayling, which lie deep in the water and will not rise, can infallibly be taken with deep-sunken grasshoppers drawn past their lurking-place; I can confidently believe in any infallible method that I have not seen tried. The Russian ecologist G. V. Nikolsky says that the grayling of the northern Urals feed on migratory shrews that swim across the rivers, and are taken on felt lures that imitate shrews.

Grayling will rise to flies on the surface on occasion (especially, it seems, when the fly has been cast by someone who hopes for trout). Some grayling specialists believe that their lateral vision is poorer, and their forward vision better than a trout's, since grayling seem to rise only to flies in a long, narrow area in front of them. Others hold that their great dorsal fins prevent them from turning as quickly as a trout, so that they prefer to move forwards to their food; though surely a grayling could lower its fin if it wanted to.

The great fin is, in fact, rather hard to explain in terms of the grayling's swimming habits; it is probably more for signalling than for propulsion, a flag not a sail. For the male grayling waves a larger fin than the female, and in the breeding season after the spring thaw the fin is most prominent, with dark spots on a purple-tinged ground. Fish can signal with their fins, not only sideways; when a spotted dorsal fin ripples, the effect seen from in front or behind is of a pair of spots leaping from side to side above the fish's body, like the warning lights on an ambulance and nearly as prominent.

A limited insight into the way fishes interpret shapes can be had by training them to choose one particular shape, say a square painted on a lever which they can press to get food, and then offering them a choice of shapes. We would suppose that a tilted square, thus ◇ , is more like an upright square than a cross ✚ is; but fish of several species including grayling unanimously disagree. It seems that fish classify objects, not according to their overall shape, but according to the features on the top and bottom; where the prominent fins are placed. Some fish may give more weight to features on the top; perhaps this is why trout ignore the hook beneath them.

The newly-caught grayling are supposed to have a smell of thyme; whence the name, *Thymallus*. The majority of those who have investigated the matter can detect no such odour; D'Arcy Thompson was driven to suppose that it was invented by some etymologist striving to explain the name. But perhaps more humans are scent-numb than are colour-blind.

An anomalous fish, then, in several ways; and indeed I am not certain it belongs in this chapter. For with its need for summer water to breed in, the grayling may not have survived the worst rigours of the last glaciation in Britain, but may have retreated further south and returned later. It is not found in Ireland, which suggests that it could not live in the very coldest unglaciated regions, and arrived in Britain too late to make the passage westwards.

For fish like grayling, that cannot survive salt water, can only have moved into Britain from Europe in the brief period between the improvement of the climate and the rise in sea level the improvement

Grayling; a rainbow reflected in beaten silver

produced. When much of the world's water lay as ice over Europe and North America, the sea stood lower all over the globe, down by as much as a hundred fathoms, or more. Britain and Ireland were then ice-shrouded peninsulas of continental Europe. As the ice melted, the seas rose; by ten thousand years ago, when the last British glaciers had retreated into the hills and pines and hazels had replaced the tundra, the sea was only forty fathoms below its present level; low enough for the North Sea to be held back further north than now, above Flamborough Head, with forests growing over the hills of the Dogger Bank and the surrounding plains. Trawlers still pull up tree-stumps from those vanished woods, through which the Rhine flowed north to the sea, with the Thames and Ouse and Trent among its tributaries. Around eight thousand five hundred years ago (when the first settled townships were forming in the Levant), the southern North Sea and the Channel were submerged, and the continent was cut off from Britain; Ireland had been separated earlier, so early that no reptiles had made their way there, nor warm-water fish except by sea.

The cold-shunning freshwater fish, then, must have come down the rivers flowing from the Continent and up their English tributaries before the seas parted them; grayling could well have been among the first to do so. The numerous summer-spawning coarse freshwater fish would have come later; many of the European species that we lack – ide, asp, schneider, nase, zope, bitterling – did not spread north in time. Some biologists hold that the coarse fish that did pass down the greater Rhine and into Britain could only have reached the eastward-draining rivers by themselves, and that their presence elsewhere is due to human aid; this is not certain.

It is true that purely freshwater fish can only move naturally between river systems if they are carried by floods across the land, or by birds or waterspouts through the air. But some coarse fish must have spread thus across the east-west watershed. I mentioned before the many species of the Brandon deposits, laid down by the westward-flowing Avon when there were no modern men to move fish; and at White Moor, near Boseley in Cheshire, floodwater deposits laid down just after the last glaciation contain the unmistakeable pharyngeal teeth of rudd. The Mesolithic Britons then had dogs and canoes, nets and harpoons; but would they have carried rudd to Cheshire?

Conceivably. The dace were probably brought to Ireland in 1899 by the sort of mistake that might have occurred in Mesolithic times. A Mr Logan had caused them to be brought from England, having heard of their virtues as live-bait, and they were left overnight in a can dangling in the Cork Blackwater. The wind blew, the rain fell, the river rose, the can was lost and the trout fishing of the Blackwater has been appreciably worse ever since. But Mesolithic man would have had to carry his pot of rudd as he walked; surely not for far.

Our "native" fishes, then, may well have reached their present abodes by their own efforts, or rather by their own submission to the accidents of history. Who can truly say what animals are native to such a changeable island, or promontory; on the showing of the last interglacial, shall we count the hippopotamus? Few have been native for more than ten thousand years; say three hours on Manfred Eigen's timescale, where all of life on earth is contracted to a centenarian's lifetime. Half that time has seen all of literate civilisation arise, and spread, and at times decay; and all in the ebb-tide of the present interglacial, since the climatic optimum from seven to five thousand years ago, after which the northern weather has chilled and the southwards retreat of sun-loving species has started. (The well-preserved shells of the European pond tortoise, *Emys orbicularis*, best mark this withdrawal of summer; once it bred as far north as Norfolk and Denmark, but now no further than France.) But there will be compensations in the gradual development of the next ice-age; for as the ice forms, the rains spread further south. Who would not exchange the dank fogs of interglacial England for a well-watered Morocco?

Legendary Monster

Jim Corbett, recounting his career as a specialist in man-eating big cats, describes an unnerving encounter with a leopard which made a kill and then lay in ambush, waiting for Corbett to be attracted to the bait. The most important thing about hunting, he remarks, is that there should be a clear understanding as to who is stalking whom. When an angler contemplates a really big pike, some of this understanding seems to become tenuous; a pike is quite obviously a serious predator, its teeth are visibly designed to inflict grievous bodily harm, and alone among freshwater fishes it looks up at the angler full-face, both calculating eyes set in its menacing mask. I think it is this sense of encountering an enemy, rather than just selecting a victim, that inspires some anglers in their obsessive devotion to the pursuit of big pike, and others in their accounts of pike impossibly big; though the limits of possibility remain uncertain, and to separate legend from truth is a delicate matter.

Of course the normal, factual pike is not really a threat to humans, and if you want the thrill of encountering a possible man-eater you should try shark-fishing in the seas off Cornwall. In inland waters, aqualung divers are routinely warned of the perils of the monster pike lurking in the deeps, and as routinely disappointed. There has only been one case of a diver being bitten by a pike, and then it was acting under a misapprehension; the diver, in the dark waters of the Norfolk broads, was wearing a black rubber suit and a gold watch, and the pike went for the shining lure, not realising that it was connected to the rest of the diver. But divers do report that pike, even if not inclined to tackle a species that must after all be much heavier than themselves, are remarkably unafraid of human intruders; they observe divers with interest and, if approached, contemptuously present their rear quarters, confident of their ability to sprint away from any possible danger.

Such confidence is entirely justified. Pike, even more than salmon or trout, are built for sudden acceleration. The long, streamlined body can produce great thrusting power; the big rounded tail, and the dorsal and anal fins set back like the flights of an arrow, transmit this power very well when lunging forward from a standing start. Startled pike can accelerate at an initial rate of eight g or more; but the big rear fins produce too much drag for the fish to swim for long at high speed. The pike's tactics, therefore, are to lurk concealed, in still water if possible, until an unwary victim comes within range of a sudden short dash; or to patrol slowly and work its way into striking distance.

The pike's colouring is admirably suited for the stealthy concealment such tactics require. Young pike have long, wavy, creamy-white stripes running up the light brownish-green flanks from the pale belly, and an unbroken dark green on the back; so camouflaged, they blend into the

Stealth, speed, skill and strength: no other fish displays the qualities of a predator more positively than the pike

reeds or the shadows of overhanging branches to the point of invisibility. (They have also an inexplicable trick of moving through reeds or other vegetation, parting the stems without causing the slightest disturbance.) As they age, the stripes break up, giving an irregular wavy boundary between flank and belly colouring, and a series of rows of roughly oval spots along the sides, as many as nine in some fish. These dappled sides may be better at blending with the shifting light under the ripples of open water where big pike can venture with more security than small ones. The fins are inconspicuous, the paired fins a uniform pale brown, the unpaired fins a greenish-yellow, occasionally with a reddish or orange tinge, with large, irregular dark blotches. Once out of water, but rarely beneath it, a pike can be seen to be flecked with gold all along its body; on the exposed tip of each body scale there is a tiny golden spot. The head, too, has an intricate pattern of golden markings. In the rare mutant silver pike this metallic beauty is taken further, in a pattern of steel blue above and silver below; conspicuous, though, and selected against in the wild.

However, what most concerns pike anglers is not the shape or colour of their quarry, but its size. In the still lakes or quiet lowland rivers where pike abound, they are the local Leviathans, in some places a compensation for the absent salmon, and only recently rivalled by monstrous carp. It is quite certain that pike grow to fifty pounds or more; the much-debated question is, how much more? and further to that question, how shall we best take great pike? There is no end to the marvellous accounts of monstrous pike; I will begin to deal with them later; let us now see what a pike makes of other fish, to understand how it may best be deceived.

Pike in the daytime in clear water hunt partly by sight. They prefer to get level with or a little below their victim, holding it in binocular vision with their large yellow eyes, before they dash forwards; so a skilful angler will aim to place his bait rather higher in the water than the depth he thinks the pike is at. But as well as sight, they rely a great deal on their ability to feel objects moving in the water, with what is usually called the lateral line, though indeed you will search a pike in vain for any visible line down its side.

This feeling of motion in the water is the most difficult of all a fish's senses for a human to appreciate; it is not the same as hearing, nor is it really like our sense of touch as applied to solid objects. Perhaps the best way to feel the sort of sensation that dominates the life of many fish is to wave your outstretched hand, just missing your face. As well as hearing the noise of your hand moving, you can feel the draught as the air displaced by your hand moves over your face. The lateral line system responds to this movement of displaced water, far more sensitively than your skin senses movements in the air, but not at all to the changes in pressure which stimulate our sense of hearing; for as a sound wave passes the molecules move together and apart, over very small distances, as the pressure rises and falls, but there is no net displacement of the water, or air, through which the wave travels.

When any solid object moves or vibrates, in water or in air, it both creates pressure waves, which can be heard as sound, and moves the water or air around it. If you are very close to the object, the pressure waves are weaker (and so less easily detected) than the displacement; but the intensity of pressure waves falls off with distance far less than the displacement does. So for an object vibrating at a particular frequency, there is a critical distance below which the pressure waves are weaker than the displacement, and above which the displacement is weaker than the pressure wave; the higher the frequency, the lower the critical distance. The critical distance also depends on the nature of the transmitting medium; it is much shorter in air than in water, which is much less compressible and so transmits displacement better. Land animals have evolved complicated ears for detecting fairly high-frequency, short-wavelength vibrations in the air, for which the critical distance is very short indeed; such ears must work as pressure-wave detectors. But in water, especially in shallow fresh waters which are often turbulent or plant-choked, vibrations are scattered very much more than in air. The least scattered, like the least scattered light in turbid waters, are the long-wavelength, low-frequency vibrations, for which the critical distance underwater may be several yards: a long way for a small fish to swim, and often further than it can see. So it is not surprising that fish all have well-developed low-frequency displacement detectors. Some have also evolved pressure-wave detectors with which they can hear sounds much as we can; we will meet them later; pike, like perch and salmonids, are deaf to our sounds.

But their displacement detectors are exquisitely sensitive. The basic elements with which they sense displacement are called the neuromast organs. These are groups of sensitive cells in the epidermis, each of which has a hair-like extension. The hairs of a neuromast organ are all inserted into a gelatinous structure called the cupola, which is about one tenth of a millimetre across and three or four times that in length, and which sticks out from the epidermis. As water around the cupola moves, the cupola bends and the hairs bend with it; when the hairs bend, they touch bundles of filaments in the sensitive cells, and cause them to stimulate the nerve that runs to the neuromast organ. The bundles of filaments are arranged on one side of the hair only, so an individual sensitive cell responds to the hair only if it moves in one particular direction. In any one neuromast organ, the bundles are placed on opposite sides of the hair in alternating cells, so that the neuromast as a whole responds to water displacement to or fro, but only in one plane. This can be shown by attaching micro-electrodes to a nerve serving an individual neuromast; the nerve sends an impulse if the cupola is bent in the plane in which the hairs and filament bundles are aligned by as little as one thousandth of a millimetre but not otherwise.

These neuromasts are too sensitive for some purposes. In a fish that lives in fast-flowing, turbulent water, or in one that spends much time swimming rapidly, neuromasts that are directly in contact with the

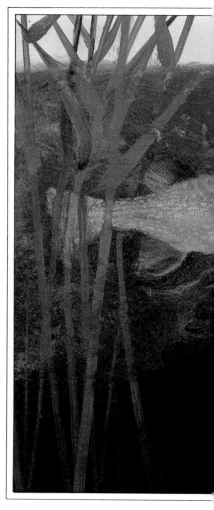

The lurking pike . . .

water around the fish would be over-stimulated; as a man exposed to a very loud continuous noise, of machinery or of an avalanche, ceases to hear even that noise, so a system of exposed neuromasts becomes deafened by too much motion of water. All fish fry, which cannot themselves move fast but need as much warning as possible of the approach of larger fishes, have exposed neuromasts, which develop in the larvae even before eyes do. But in most species many of the neuromasts become enclosed, as the fish develops, in a series of channels under the skin. The cupolas of these enclosed neuromasts extend across the channel, and each channel is connected to the water outside by a series of pores; so the enclosed neuromasts are much less sensitive to displacement of the water outside, but can still function against the noise of rushing water. Several such channels run across the head, and along the upper and lower jaws; but the most prominent run in most fish back from the head, on either side, and down the flanks towards the tail, often with an upward loop to keep clear of the turbulence around the pectoral fin. From their position, these are called the lateral lines; and the whole system of neuromasts is sometimes called the lateral line system.

But pike do not inhabit turbulent water, and except in the few seconds of their attacking or escaping dash they do not swim fast; so

. . . suddenly strikes

they do not need to muffle their neuromasts. Therefore they have no visible lateral line, no system of channels and pores. Their equivalent of the lateral line is a row of open shallow pits, each containing a row of exposed neuromasts; each pit lies in a notch in the front edge of a scale. There is a series of such pits running along each side of a pike, in the position of the lateral line of other fishes; but there are also other series of pits, above and below, arranged in horizontal or vertical rows. When the pits are viewed under the microscope, one can see that the neuromasts in the vertical rows are sensitive to vertical displacement of the water, and those in the horizontal rows to horizontal displacements. This is an admirable design for obtaining the precise range, speed and bearing of any moving underwater object; for the waves of displacement that such an object causes will reach different elements of the system at different times, according to its range and so on, and the vertical and horizontal rows make it possible to get a fix in two planes simultaneously, like the crosswires in a gunsight, or like the soundranging systems of some owls which have one ear opening tall and narrow and the other short and wide, so as to plot the source of sound on two co-ordinates.

A pike lying quietly in the water can detect the approach of its prey, or of a rival, even in the dark, with more sensitivity than most other fishes can. It is not certain how sensitive the pike's rangefinding is; experiments with blinded pike have shown that they will snap accurately at a moving bait only when it gets to within four inches of them. Maybe they can locate moving objects at much longer ranges, but prefer to keep still; for the drawback of the pike's exposed, sensitive neuromasts is that the whole system must be deafened as soon as the pike starts to lunge through the water. Therefore a pike that has located a possible prey must either be able to rely on its vision to follow the prey's movements in the last stages of the attack, or let the prey get so close that it has no time to take evasive action. A blinded pike, or a pike in the dark, that lunged out at a moving prey some feet away would have to aim for where it thought the prey was heading for, and would have no information from its deafened neuromasts after it started its lunge. Prey species have their own lateral lines, and those that continue moving in a straight line after they have detected a pike coming at them are rather strongly selected against.

A pike has to judge the position of its prey very accurately, for when it strikes the long grinning mouth is less efficient at sucking in the prey than a perch's rounded protrusible gape, because water is sucked in through the sides of the grin as well as from the front. But on the other hand, the pike's long jaws can seize the prey from any angle, while the perch can only grasp its victim end-on. Pike seem to prefer to strike sideways on (perhaps because a fish sideways on is sucked in more easily), and to hold the prey crossways in their jaws for a while, as their large lower teeth deal it incapacitating wounds. The numerous, smaller upper teeth are mounted elastically in the palate; they can easily be bent back to allow food to pass down the gullet, but resist its efforts to escape. A pike will often swim with its victim into open water, or into its own holt – that is, to a place from which a lively victim is unlikely to escape – before releasing the crosswise grip and swallowing the prey head-first.

Anglers for generations have been endeavouring to persuade pike to launch their attacks at a concealed hook; with an early appreciation of the pike's two bites at the target, which has led some to practise striking fast and hard at the moment of the first bite - when the bait is, after all, within the fish's jaws - and others of a more cautious disposition to wait for the second, headways bite lest their belated strike coincide with the pike's temporary release of the bait. (A few unsporting characters have taken no chances and waited till the bait is well and truly swallowed, which does at least ensure the death of the pike even if you lose it. This practice of "gorging" is now frowned upon.)

Pike do not even disdain worms; nothing that seems approximately edible comes amiss to them. (A twenty-eight-pound pike was taken in the Ouse, in 1765, that had in its belly the fob watch of a recently drowned gentleman; who knows what the pike took it for? Sharks are even less discriminating, as witness the eighteenth-century American sea-captain, ungrateful for the benefits of British rule, who set up as a privateer, duly certified as such. Encountering one of His Majesty's warships, he threw the incriminating certificates overboard and reverted to his former status of loyal merchant; which pretence he maintained till some sailors on another ship, passing their time off duty in a little angling, hauled in a great shark and found enough evidence in its belly to hang him.)

But for a reliable, everyday bait for pike an angler needs something which will attract pike only. A much bigger live-bait than a worm is needed; roach or dace or perch have long been favourites. They may be tethered with a single large hook through the lip or, much more reliably, with one of the varieties of snap-tackle that have replaced the laboriously sewn-in hooks of Walton's day.

Instead of being live, baits may as well be dead, if not completely artificial. For many years anglers have supposed that the important part of taking a pike with a bait that is not alive is to persuade the pike otherwise; so dead fish have been threaded through the mouth with a hook at the rear, then artfully cast out, allowed to sink, and drawn up to the surface with an enticing flutter; or fixed to a spinning vane and drawn along through the water. Both techniques work, sometimes. The chaotic turbulence that the dead bait produces as it moves must be perceived by the pike's neuromasts as something extraordinary, which perhaps attracts some and frightens others. An additional improvement, said to be particularly effective with perch as a dead bait, is to remove several scales from the sides to create white patches; the idea is to make the pike think that the bait is infected with fungus and will therefore be easy meat.

In fact, pike turn out to prefer even easier meat if they can get it, a dead fish lying on the bottom (which is also a more natural, and so a more deceptive, position).

This was once common knowledge; listen to the *Boke of St Albans*:

> *The Pike is a good fish; but for that he devoureth so many as well of his own kind as of other, I love him the less. And for to take him you shall do this. Take a codling hook* (that is, a hook suitable for taking small cod) *and take a roach or a fresh herring, and a wire with a hole in the end, and put it in at the mouth and out at the tail, down by the ridge of the fresh herring; and then put the hook in after, and draw the hook into the cheek of the fresh herring; then put a plumb of lead upon your line a yard long from your hook, and a float in midway between; and cast it in a pit where the pike useth, and this is the best and most surest craft of taking the pike.*

This is uncommonly sound advice; as was proved over four centuries after it was published, in 1954, when Mr Fred J. Taylor of Aylesbury resurrected the art of stationary dead-bait pikefishing, with enormous effect. Various improvements have been made in fixing the hooks, so as to ensure a more certain strike; but herring remains the favourite bait. Roach or rudd are preferred over weedy or very muddy bottoms, since their swim-bladders still provide lift after their death and the bait does not sink in; herrings' bladders collapse. In the normal way of things pike do not come across herring; though they do in the brackish waters of the Baltic, a melted glacier not yet mixed with the salt Atlantic, where pike swim miles from land and feed on strange meats. But English pike seem to like the taste, too; probably the oily flavour carries well. The herring does not have to be overwhelmingly fresh, quite the reverse. In picking up such bait, pike must rely on their sense of smell rather than sight or vibration, and this may be one of the things attracting them to moving dead-bait or even live-bait.

With such a killing method known, why did pike fishers ever abandon it? I think it was, in part, a case of technological infatuation, after spinning with a reel was invented. Stationary dead-baiting without a reel, or tethered live-baiting, is easy, but a reel makes all sorts of spinning artifices possible. The reel first appears in *The Art of Angling, wherein are discovered many rare secrets, very necessary to be known by all that delight in that recreation*, by Thomas Barker, an Ancient Practicioner in the said Art, who anticipated Walton's first edition by a couple of years. Barker was a cook by profession, and his attitude to angling was sometimes dictated by the cook's need to have raw materials no matter how they are got. A speedy way to take pike, he says, is to put the sharpest, heaviest hook you have on the end of six or eight feet of line, and "when Pike go a-frogging up ditches, and in the river to sun them, as in May, June and July . . . you may strike the Pike you see with the bare hook where you please; this Line and Hook doth far exceed snaring", however far it falls short of angling.

But when Barker was in his mood for recreation, he used more sporting techniques; and was perhaps inclined to use complicated gadgets through his experience in kitchens (where he was also a master of his craft, "admitted into the most Ambassador's kitchens that have come into England these forty years, and do wait on them still at the Lord Protector's charge"). He used to angle for trout with a minnow, placed on the hook so as to twist in the stream, and drawn up the river; this is the embryonic form of spinning, and Barker was the first to mention the essential technical improvement of putting a swivel in the line to stop it twisting. Once the swivel had been devised, it became possible to use a reel; Barker says that this was done by a namesake of his, who wagered that he could take a pike four feet long within one month's angling. He had "a Hazel Rod of twelve feet long, with a ring of wyre in the top of his rod, for his Line to run through; within two foot of the bottom of the Rod, there was a hole made for to put in a wind, to turn with a barrell, to gather up his Line and loose it at his pleasure." He won the bet with three days to spare.

Reels spread slowly; it is doubtful that Walton ever used one, though he knew of their use in salmon-fishing. "To be observed better by seeing one of them, than by a large demonstration of words", he said, evading a tedious difficulty familiar to all writers of technical manuals. But they quite changed pike-fishing; "trolling", the new method was called, though we now use that word mostly for pulling a bait from a moving boat, and speak otherwise of "spinning". The Reverend Robert Nobbes, M.A., Vicar of Applethorpe and Wood Newton in the county of Northampton, one of the long line of fishing clerics that started with St Peter, published in 1682 *The Complete Troller*, and thus became the first recorded pike specialist. His book deals only with pike, and considers trolling as the only proper method of taking them; dace, gudgeon and roach are his favourite baits. I think the attraction of spinning with a reel must then have lain wholly in the way it lets the angler search out the parts of the water he chooses, imposing his will on the fish rather than waiting for it to come to him. The modern artificial spinning baits, spoons and plugs and minnows that look so ingenious and deceive the pike most thoroughly, are a later attraction. Walton, it is true, carried with him an artificial minnow, of coloured silk on a cloth body, for use if a real one was not to be had, but that was not for spinning.

Of course, like all new ideas, trolling met some ridicule. *A Song against Fishing*, by one Dr Martin Lluelyn, has great verve if shaky grammar:

> *Hooks and lines of larger sizes*
> *Such that the Tyrant that Trolls devises,*
> *Fishes ne'er, believe his fable,*
> *What he calls a Line's a Cable.*
> *That's a Knave of endless rancour*
> *Who for a Hook casts in an Anchor.*

The learned Doctor's criticism, from as early as 1646, has been echoed since. Trolling for big pike does require substantial, inelegant gear. If you want a big fish you need a fair-sized bait, and big spinners are definitely ironmongery. Furthermore, any method of pike fishing needs a wire trace between the hook and the line, or the pike's teeth will win its freedom easily; taking a fish with such machinery is the very opposite of playing a trout with a minute fly mounted on a single horse-hair, as Barker in his more sporting moments could do.

I wonder, incidentally, how much pike fishing may have been encouraged by improvements in the mediaeval armament industry. Pike was once a most expensive dish; in Edward I's time, twice as costly as salmon and ten times more than turbot. In those days, metal wires could only be made by hand, usually by hammering out an ingot into successively thinner rods: a wearisome and costly business. Most of the wire so made went into chain-mail, an expensive necessity for the nobility. During the fourteenth century some unknown armourer, probably in Germany, improved the technique of wire-drawing, in

Deadbait. A small dace made formidable by the addition of steel teeth.

which a continuous thread of metal is pulled through an aperture, and arranged to have the process driven by water-power; the price of chain-mail collapsed, and angling for pike must have become far less expensive.

That aside, the gear for spinning for pike is not, and cannot be, delicately made; but there are subtleties in its use as delicate as any in fly-fishing. Especially with the modern plug baits, plastic or wooden lures that are shaped and patterned like a rather nondescript small fish, an expert can achieve marvels; for with jointed bodies and angled lips at the front, they can be made to dive or rise in the water by altering the rate of recovery, and can be steered over obstructions and below overhangs to search out the suspected, or known, haunts of pike. The old-fashioned spoons and minnows (sometimes called Devons, from the incomparably beautiful county of their origin) probably cause more turbulence as they are spun, but can be controlled less.

A pike making for such a bait can be guided only by the displacement of the water, or by sight. The makers of spinning baits usually go to some trouble to give them a scaly surface, fish-like markings, prominent eyes; even, sometimes, on Devon minnows where the whole body revolves as it moves and all details must be hopelessly blurred. Many anglers swear that their favourite plug has gone on taking pike after successive teeth had chipped the paint away; so it is probably the

A good afternoon's sport in January. These are the biggest of seven pike, totalling 60 pounds, swapped for three bottles of Côtes du Rhône

movement, not the colour, the pike go for. But some lures nevertheless attempt elaborate deceptions; there are mechanical marvels that imitate swimming frogs (but perhaps catch more anglers than pike). Mr Fred Buller, the outstanding luciophile of his generation, once had an imitation rat plug made, of musk-rat fur over a polystyrene body with a strip of sealskin for tail, to entrap the pike of a pond where rats were a major part of the diet; I do not know if he had heard of the calf's-tail bait, trimmed to resemble a water-rat, used in the last century as a good winter bait for pike.

An old method for increasing the zone searched by a bait, now in discredit except among exterminatory bailiffs of trout waters, is the trimmer; a very large float, with bait attached, set free to drift across the water. There is no art in using such a method, except in attaching the bait so that a hard pull as the pike starts to run will release several fathoms of line, so that the float will not be pulled under. This method has had its glories, if an account in *The Field*, as issued on 7th September 1901, is to be believed. Some Irish sportsmen are said to have seen a duck disappear unnaturally under the waters of Lough Sheelan and deduced the presence of a great pike. They set loose an improvised trimmer, a spoon bait attached to a barrel, blown by the wind across the lough; the pike towed the barrel for eighty minutes before they could retrieve it, and on being taken was found to measure four feet five and three quarter inches and to weigh fifty-three pounds eleven ounces. If true, this would be bigger than any legitimately caught pike in Britain. If; but eighty minutes is a suspiciously short time. When Colonel Thornton took his forty-nine-pound pike on Loch Patuliche, in 1784, it towed a rowing boat bearing himself, Captain Waller, and two servants; and it took them an hour and a quarter before the servants could wade in and draw the monster ashore by its tail.

A form of trimming now extinct, which would nowadays bring down the justified wrath of the Royal Society for the Prevention of Cruelty to Animals on all concerned, was to tie the bait to a goose's leg and set the goose free on a pike-infested lake. "And if ye list to have a good sport," says the *Boke of St Albans*, "then tye the cord to a goose's foot, and ye shall see good hauling whether the goose or the pike shall haul the better." This passage is one that suggests that the *Boke* might perhaps not have been written by an abbess. But the unquestionably Reverend W.B. Daniel, whose *Rural Sports* of 1801 is an encyclopedia of pre-industrial England, speaks of the same practice, and adds the valuable information that you can safely bet on the goose.

Yet more idiosyncratic methods have had occasional success. A fine, forty-pound, forty-nine-inch pike was landed in the grounds of Upton House, near Edgehill, in the summer of 1865 by the gallant Colonel Purefoy Fitzgerald; he had observed it to seize the head of a floating croquet mallet, thrown into the lake on the end of a string by his three-year-old son. The great pike of Whittlesea Mere, the biggest known in England, fifty-two (or possibly only forty-nine) pounds, had been taken fourteen years before by an even more unrepeatable method; they dug a fifteen-mile canal and drained the Mere. And there is the story, of uncertain provenance, of the pike found dead in a haystack, his teeth set firm in the hind leg of a dead fox; but I know of no imitation fox plugs.

As for the timing of your pike fishing; pike breed early in the year for coarse fish, from March to May, so that their offspring can grow and feed on the plentiful young of coarser summer-spawning species. They feed happily through the winter, even in snow and ice; they are more easily taken in the cold weather when the weeds have died down, and sybaritic anglers reckon November, when much of the encumbering growth has gone but the weather is still kind to humans, to be the best time. Dedicated souls neglect such considerations.

A coursing pike

And as for the best time of day to angle for pike; it is certain that they are, in some waters at least, more active in the dark than in the day. Their daily round has been most extensively studied in the lakes of Manitoba, where Dr G.H. Lawler set gill-nets at different depths and hauled them up at intervals so as to sample the movements of pike. He found that, in water less than two metres deep, pike were on average most active during the hours of darkness (about 6.30 pm to 5.30 am at the time of his labours); as the sun rose, the pike catch in shallow water fell to a fifth of its night-time level. After about 10 am pike began to return to the shallows; by late afternoon they were three times as abundant as in the early morning, and the greatest number were netted just after dark. But with deep-set nets the story was different; here, pike were netted as they swam at night, but the catch rose sharply after sunrise.

These daily migrations may be, in part, due to the pike sensibly following their prey. Coarse fish generally have a well-acknowledged tendency to forage in shallow water at night, when they are safe from fish-eating birds, and to shelter in deeper water soon after sunrise. (In some parts of the world there are fish-eating bats, which use their high-frequency echo-sounders to detect the ripples made by fishes close to the surface, and swoop on them in the darkness; there are none such in England, and I cannot say how their presence affects the night life of fish elsewhere.) But the return to shallow water in the afternoon is odd: most fish have their day arranged symmetrically around noon.

If the pike of England behave like those of Manitoba then we can draw two morals. One is that night-time margin fishing for pike, with stationary dead-bait or tethered live-bait, might be very rewarding. The other, that if you prefer to spin for pike, you stand a much better chance in the late afternoon than in the morning, and can lie in bed with a clear conscience.

And when, by whatever means, you have caught your pike, there are only three things you can do with it. If you have gaffed it carefully, in the loose skin between the lower jawbones, you can remove the hook and return it to the water without more ado; if you have mastered the art of using a pike gag and a hook disgorger you can also have intact fingers. Or you may consider the pike worth cooking, as it certainly is, far above the usual run of coarse fish on which it has fed. Walton himself has a famously mouth-watering recipe for roast pike, "a dish of meat too good for any but anglers, or very honest men"; I will not deprive you of the pleasure of reading it yourself, but I will mention in passing that the only oranges Walton knew were the bitter Seville kind, hard to find out of season in England nowadays, not the modern sweet juicy ones. They do say that his recipe works much better if you use lemon-juice instead.

Also, Walton calls for a fair-sized pike, and you may wish to cook something more moderate. There is an excellent sauce for all delicate-flavoured fish, the *beurre blanc* of the Loire valley, which goes excellently with pike. The sauce itself requires a little practice; but the recipe calls for rather less than a bottle of dry Loire wine, so you have room for mistakes and consolation.

Gut and scale the pike. Simmer together half a bottle of dry white wine, with the same amount of water, a sliced carrot, a sliced shallot, seasoning to taste, and maybe a slice of celery, for half an hour or so, then poach the pike in the strained liquid, a quarter of an hour for four pounds weight. While it is cooking, chop up more shallots very fine, and cook gently in a small pan with, for each shallot, another tablespoon of the wine and one of vinegar. When they are soft and the sauce is only just liquid, put the pan aside and leave to cool till the fish is ready. Then re-heat very gently and add two ounces of unsalted butter for each shallot, a little at a time, whisking it in and never letting it completely melt, till in a minute or so you have a creamy sauce to serve with the drained fish.

In Anjou, where the sauce has its first home, they use Muscadet or some such light dry wine. In Touraine they cheat, by Angevin standards, by replacing a little of the butter by thick cream, which makes the sauce easier for the less skilful; also they have the excellent white wine of Vouvray which improves any fish dish.

There are other recipes for stuffed pike; but the recipe which every pike specialist dreams of involves the biggest pike in the world, stuffed with sawdust and mounted over his mantlepiece. And the third course of action, tempting to anyone who takes a big pike, is to preserve the specimen; and then to argue about how much bigger it might have been.

This argument is always inconclusive; pike have a notable tendency to grow after their death. Sometimes this growth is measurable, as in the case of the forty-three-pound "record British rod-caught pike" of 1974, which turned out to have been only thirty-two pounds before taxidermy. Further, there is a difference between the size of officially recognised captures, the size of larger fish which probably (or certainly) existed but fail to be officially recognised, and the alluring tales of even bigger fish which perhaps cannot be definitely disproved. For instance, it is not seriously in doubt that Mr John Garvin took a fifty-three-pound pike from Lough Conn in July 1920, the biggest rod-caught specimen of this century in Britain (if you count Ireland as one of the British Isles); but he did not document its capture in the manner now deemed necessary, forgivably since there was a civil war at the time, and it is no longer the acknowledged record, though it is undoubted evidence that pike over fifty pounds are to be found. But when it comes to pike more distant in time or space, the documentation is inevitably more questionable. Like the mythical figures that haunt Auden's odes,

> *Yes, they were living here once but do not now,*
> *Yes, they are living still but do not here . . .*

the truly monstrous pike are never easily accessible. The trouble is, there are excellent reasons for supposing that pike were bigger in the past, and in more distant waters, than those on our local waters today.

Of course, some of the stories are plainly false. Pliny, the father of lies and of popular encyclopaedias of natural history, mentions the great river fish *Esox* that can grow to a thousand pounds; the modern pike, *Esox lucius*, keeps within three figures at most. The great pike of Mannheim, whose story Walton cites from Gessner, was supposedly taken in 1497; it was said to weigh three hundred and fifty pounds, or some say five hundred and fifty, and to have been caught with a ring round its gill bearing a Greek inscription made for the Emperor Frederick II, dating from 1230. The detail of the ring alone would be enough to convince me that the story must be false: for I first came across it told of Charles VI of France, in the misty forests of the middle ages capturing a great stag, whose golden collar read *Caesar mihi hoc dedit*, Caesar gave me this; then as a ring of James I and VI, supposedly found decorating an aged falcon in South Africa; and at last I traced it to (inevitably) Pliny, who also makes it a stag's collar but names Alexander the Great as donor. Furthermore, the pike's skeleton preserved in Mannheim Cathedral is impossibly long for the supposed weight and has been reinforced by the vertebrae of several extra pike. I suppose that leaves it a possibility that the original unimproved specimen may have been quite big.

Mr Fred Buller, in his memorable book on pike, has published his famous *Big Pike List* of possible British monsters, headed by the sixty-pound fish found dying in Dowdeswell Reservoir near Cheltenham in 1896, and the seventy-two-pound Loch Ken pike taken on a peacock-feather fly – or possibly on a trimmer baited with a duck, according to another tradition – in 1774 or thereabouts. The biggest claim for a British pike that I have come across in print is the seven-foot, one hundred-and-seventy-pound specimen which Daniel says was taken from a pool nine yards deep at Lillishall Limeworks, near Newport, Monmouth, in January 1765. The story is highly dubious; for it is alleged both that the pool had not been fished in living memory, and also that the Clerk of the Parish had earlier been pulled into it while trolling, and at least one of these statements must be false. Also, the catch was not reported in print till over thirty years later, which gives plenty of time for posthumous growth. And furthermore, the alleged captors were Welshmen, and as such were likely to have had their poetical imagination highly developed. This has been so since time immemorial; I cannot do better than cite Giraldus Cambrensis, himself of Welsh birth, who in the twelfth century noted that the table conversation or public speaking of an ordinary Welshman would be thought remarkable eloquence in England, but that his testimony was likely to be shaped by rhetoric rather than facts.

Giraldus's reliability may be tested by his description of the Irish. In the coronation of the kings of Ulster, he asserts, the king copulates with a mare; the beast is then killed and made into a stew, the king bathes in the stew and the horseflesh is then eaten at the banquet. I told my Irish brother-in-law of this account, and after some thought he agreed it was probably true. The O'Neills, he explained, are capable of anything.

That most of the very big British pike come from the lakes of Scotland and Ireland, however, has nothing to do with the Celtic twilight. Pike will grow large if they have lots of food, and for very big pike that means lots of big prey, sizeable trout and salmon; lochs and loughs will provide these in abundance, while in the over-fished waters of over-populated England pike must make do with smaller fish that collectively require more effort in pursuit. A seventy-eight-pound pike, even bigger than the Loch Ken monster, is said to have been taken by a Mr O'Hanagan in County Clare, in August 1830. The angler was in his seventieth year, but then his compatriot Mr Purcell, of County Cork, was even older when in 1811 he was knighted for killing three burglars with a carving knife.

Probably the days of the very big Irish pike were prolonged by the general indifference to angling in that country; nowadays, the Inland Fisheries Trust has reduced the numbers of pike in a deliberate effort to favour game fish and attract tourists, netting several giants over forty pounds in the process. (The lack of native fishermen remains, to the benefit of visitors: "If I could be born again," said a German angler, interviewed on Irish television, "I would be a turbot off the coast of Connaught; I'd eat fresh shellfish every day, and I'd live for ever".) But

Overleaf
A monster of forty pounds taking an angler's live-bait, ensuring a very lively struggle for both parties, as long as the tackle holds

some Irish monsters may remain; Mr Clive Gammon has a celebrated recipe for taking a record pike: first win the pools, then buy an Irish estate with a sizeable private lough that has not been fished for generations, and then. . .

This need of big pike for big, rich, unfished waters is the reason why the credible accounts of enormous ones come from parts of the northern hemisphere with very big lakes and rivers and, till recently, little population; far away and often long ago; sometimes no more than travellers' tales, which are proverbially in the same class as anglers' accounts; but several foreign pike are well-attested monsters. The Western European authenticated rod-caught record is no more than fifty-two pounds four ounces, taken from a gravel-pit near Goslau in the Federal Republic of Germany in 1971 by the fortunate Herr Friedrich Witzany; though the Germans speak of the great pike of Dachau Maas, a belated casualty of the First World War, as much bigger. It appears that a farmer, returned from the war, was putting his property to rights in early 1919, and found a case of explosives in his barn, abandoned from some training exercise. Being familiar with such materials, and wanting to dispose of them safely, he attached a fuse and detonator and lowered them into the depths of the nearby lake. After the expected explosion, there was a second eruption, and much thrashing on the surface; and the farmer fetched ropes and tackle and was able to drag an expiring pike longer than himself to the bank. Unfortunately, 1919 was a hungry year in Germany, and he sold his catch at once; there is no definite evidence of its size, but reports put it at around seventy pounds.

Dachau Maas is now in Poland, pending the next partition; the Poles are well aware of the pike's rapacity (their equivalent of a bull in a china shop, or a fox in a hen-roost, is a pike in a carp pond) but have produced no claims of giant pike that I know of. The Russians have; N.V. Khrostov, a trained biologist, claimed that he personally saw a thirty-four kilogram (sixty-nine pound) pike taken from Lake Il'men near Novgorod in 1930, and L.S. Berg, author of the standard guide to Soviet freshwater species, reports specimens of up to sixty-five kilograms (one hundred and thirty-one pounds) taken in the lower Dniepr in the last century. Such pike are not incredible; Lake Il'men would appear to be a coarse angler's paradise, and doubtless a pike's too: thirty miles across, with six-kilo bream and fifteen-kilo pike-perch also recorded; weights that would be respectable in Britain in pounds. At least, it yielded such fish in the thirties; but that was after only fifty years of Russian industrialisation; I would not guarantee its state today.

Further east, the Amur River basin between China and the USSR has a distinct species of pike, *Esox reicherti*, which has a reversed coat colouration, dark spots on a light background; this is no monster but is said to be the strongest for its size of any pike. Further east yet, North America boasts five species of pike. Three, the pickerels, are small; one, formerly *Esox estor*, the northern pike, is now realised to be the same as the *E. lucius* of Europe and Asia (apart from the burbot, the only purely freshwater fish to be native to both land masses). The fifth, perhaps the greatest of all pikes, is the famous muskellunge, *E. masquinongy*, of the Great Lakes, the Ohio and the St·Lawrence; the accredited rod-caught record for muskies is sixty-nine pounds fifteen ounces, and ones of over one hundred pounds and six feet have been netted. Like the Amur pike, its colouration is reversed; unlike other pike, it has no scales on the lower half of its cheek or gill-cover. Muskies are reckoned fiercer fighters than ordinary pike, too; but in competition with *E. lucius* they do badly, for they spawn later and their fry are eaten. Hybrids are known, called tiger muskies from their dark stripes; but they are not fertile.

The known size of the muskellunge, though, is no greater than the reported size of big European pike from comparable waters; so I am inclined to regard hundred-pound European pike as not intrinsically incredible. It is hard to say, really, what factors could limit the size of pike. Food supply, obviously; the effect of good feeding was shown by the Dowdeswell pike, which was said to have been put into the trout-stocked reservoir ten years before it was caught, by a local angler with a grudge against the town councillors to whom the fishing rights were restricted. In the reservoir it would have had no competition, save from the relatively ineffectual council; and the rings of its gill-covers show that it was fourteen when it died, and greatly increased its growth-rate after the age of four. A great deal of food must be needed for a monster; it has been calculated that a twelve-year-old twenty-pound pike will have eaten in its lifetime about two thousand five hundred other fish with a combined weight of three hundred and eighty pounds, and bigger pike must grow more slowly and eat yet more. But there are places like Lake Il'men where the food supply is enormous. And a big pike must have a faster top speed, and be able to dart across a greater distance, than a small one; perhaps its neuromast system can detect prey at a longer range; certainly it can cope with prey that would escape a smaller pike.

But food is not all, not even for a rapacious fish. There is an odd phenomenon which fish biologists call "the size hierarchy effect"; even if fish are provided with more food than they can eat, a big fish will grow faster if it is in the company of others of the same species, smaller than itself, than if it is alone; and a small fish grows slower in the company of big ones than if alone. It seems reasonable that a small fish would have to spend extra energy getting out of the way of big ones, but why a big fish is encouraged to grow by the sight of its inferiors is a mystery. The size hierarchy effect is best established in schooling fish; pike are to a considerable extent solitary outside the spawning season, but are presumably aware of the presence of other pike in the same water. (Some anglers believe that pike in lakes may flock together for a concerted attack on a school of prey.) They may, then, respond to size dominance: if so, then the growth rate of very large pike would be faster than one would predict from studies of average pike.

But one factor must limit the size reached by any fish; old age and its debilities. Some suppose that older pike must be more susceptible to diseases. There is a certain amount of evidence for this. The Russian biologist Gorbunova studied the abundance of twenty-one kinds of pike parasite in fish of various ages; eleven species were more common in older fish, two were rarer, nine were not affected by ageing. She suggested several reasons for her findings: older pike have a bigger area of skin and gill and are therefore more at risk from parasites that attach themselves externally; they eat more food, and so are more vulnerable to internal infection; they can catch bigger prey, and therefore risk acquiring additional parasites from them; and only older pike can develop infestations of parasites that themselves have a long life-cycle. But, intriguingly, she found some evidence that in very large, old fish (pike among other species) the intensity of parasites is reduced. Perhaps only lucky fish that escape parasites live to be old; or perhaps they become gradually immune.

It may be that in some places pike grow old faster than in others. The big pike of the Irish loughs grow with astonishing speed (one of forty-one pounds had only eight annual rings on its gill-covers) but few have been found older than twelve. Mr Garvin's fifty-two-pounder was fourteen, perhaps fifteen. But the pike of Lake Windermere, which like the Irish pike have been extensively netted and studied by fisheries biologists, reach smaller sizes, thirty to thirty-five pounds or so, and take longer to reach them, twelve to eighteen years. A pessimist would say that the big Irish pike reach the biggest size their waters will support after a dozen years, then die; or that there is a culminating size, reached sooner or later, after which old age sets in. An optimist would hope that some pike, given enough food, keep on growing at Irish rates for twenty years or longer.

As usual, the great old tyrants among pike are female. There is one possible exception; if Mr R. Brookes' *Art of Angling* (London, 1772; illustrated with 133 Cutts) is to be believed, a pair of spawning pike were taken from a ditch near Wallingford, the female of fifty-four and the male of fifty-one pounds. But I doubt if their capture was fair angling. The Thames has nothing to match them in these degenerate days; though Daniel's *Rural Sports* does record the pike taken from that river near Wytham Brook by a Mr Bishop of Godstow, which "was four feet two inches long, two feet ten inches in girth, and after being disgorged of a barbel nearly six, and a chub upwards of three pounds, weighed thirty-one pounds and a half". Yes, they were living here once but do not now . . .

CHUB

The Pursuit of the Uneatable

The chub is an excellent fish for an angler in all ways save one. It is a fish for all seasons and all styles; it will feed in cold weather, even in the snow, as well as any other, and on a hot summer's day it will still be feeding when all other fish, except the rudd, have taken their siesta. Bright sunshine will not discourage it either, and it will feed at the top or the middle or the bottom of the swim, and it will attack a great variety of baits enthusiastically, though not quite indiscriminately. So you can pursue your chub by whatever means you please, even in weather which seems perfect for haymaking or holiday-makers but is otherwise less pleasing to anglers. It is not an easy fish to catch; you may perhaps take one by random trawling in midstream after who knows what, but if you set out determined to catch a large chub you must take uncommon care. A chub is the most circumspect, or perhaps circumaudient, of fishes; it has excellent sight and probably the best hearing for its size of any fish in England, and no wonder, for it has in a sense the biggest ear.

A fish with ears as long as a hare's would be worth seeing, and no-one would be surprised if it were as wary as a hare; but to look at a chub one would not suppose that it had any ears at all. A rounded face, after which plump cheeks are called chubby; the single dorsal fin, and high pectorals with lower pelvics set far back, and the large scales that are common to all the cyprinids; a long body for a cyprinid, for it will live in rivers of moderate speed as well as in still water, and needs some power in its swimming; but where are its great ears?

Hidden inside, together with the innumerable small sharp bones that make the chub almost inedible. If the mark of a sportsman is to love the sport for its own sake, then the chub and barbel fanciers are the purest sportsmen of any anglers; more so than the heroes who stand waist-deep in icy torrents struggling with salmon, or the perfect tiers and casters who can imitate their chosen fly and get even the sex right, and drop it to the inch over the trout's nose; for they will enjoy their catch on the table. But the chub is watery and tasteless and bone-riddled, and the barbel, though the best fighter for its weight of any coarse fish, can be downright poisonous; nobody would pursue them except for purely sporting motives.

I have heard this assertion of the moral superiority of chub and barbel fishers quite often, mostly from themselves. But I fancy Walton would not have agreed with them; for the first fish that Piscator taught Venator to catch was a chub, which argues that no great skill is needed to take them; and surely Piscator cooked their catch and made a fine meal of it?

So it seems on the surface at least; but anglers should look deeper. Consider; it was a sunny day in May, past the early morning, when those anglers set out to a river that held both chub and trout, and the trout would not have been biting till evening; but Piscator knew a deep tree-shadowed hole with twenty chub in it, and knowing where to fish is more than half the secret. Then again, they caught their chub by dapping with grasshoppers, hiding themselves behind trees and lowering the bait to the surface as slowly as a snail moves. Now if you do this very carefully, making no noise and letting nothing but the bait touch the surface, it is a nearly infallible way of catching chub on a bright day; it needs no skill in casting or striking, and must have been even easier with the long sixteen-foot reelless rods of Walton's day; an encouraging method for a beginner to use, then, if he has someone else to tell him where to fish and if he has the natural virtues of an angler. I mean, if he is naturally patient, observant, quick to learn and able to keep quiet when necessary. I should not wonder if Piscator – an experienced angler and therefore deeply cunning, though most straightforward in his dealings – had not sent his new friend to dap for chub to see if he had the right spirit; for there are some agreeable companions who have rather the instincts of a harpooner, who will dash with great force and speed at any hazard and will put down every chub for miles.

And as for cooking the chub; well, Walton's recipe is doubtless the best that could be done. Any coarse fish is the better for being carefully cleaned and cooked very fresh as he recommends; and the butter and vinegar he used would fatten and flavour watery meat; but I wonder what he did about the bones? In those days carving was a gentleman's accomplishment, and it is to be noted that they had caught a very large chub which would have had more space for flesh between the spikes. But it is also to be noted that when his pupil caught a second chub, Piscator gave it away and caught some trout for their next meal. Perhaps it is no accident that the chub has more aliases than any other British freshwater fish; for a fishmonger or cook might well need to disguise him.

These aliases among fish can be most confusing. Some travellers may tell you that they have eaten chub and found it delicious and no more bony than a trout. They will turn out to have eaten it in Canada or the northern United States, where various salmonids related to our whitefish are caught under the name of "lake herring" and sold as "chub". I do not understand the marketing psychology behind this.

But in England the other common name for chub, in the south, is chavender, or sometimes cheven; like chub, both come ultimately from the late Latin *capitem*, a head; for the chub's big head is a clear distinguishing mark, hence his scientific name *Squalus* (or sometimes *Leuciscus*) *cephalus*; and similarly in French his name is *testard*, from *testa*, originally meaning a pot, hence a head in the very late Latin slang which gave birth to French. (But a testicle is probably a little witness, not a little pot.) Usually, *le vilain testard*, for the nation of gastronomes think poorly of the chub. Some say that the name may also refer to the fact that the jaw muscles around the head are boneless and therefore the least inedible part. Another name is "alderman" from his jowly appearance;

or, in the North of England, "skelly"; perhaps short for skeleton, the most impressive thing about this fish.

As for recipes for dealing with chub; Frank Buckland, a great ichthyologist of the last century, gave the best. To display the skeleton fully articulated in all its complexity, put your chub in a box with some gentles or, even better, an ants' nest. After a while, no more than ten days in a warm summer, the flesh will be all gone and you can astonish your friends by hanging up the remains.

Among the bones that can be seen if the preparation is done very carefully are the Weberian ossicles; three small bones on either side, behind the skull and below the backbone, that were once ribs but are now part of the hearing system. They are the distinguishing mark of the cyprinids (the carp-like fishes) and their relatives the silurid catfish. They connect the inner ears within the skull to the swim-bladder, which in these fish is not only a balancing organ but also a sound receptor, or more accurately a transducer. The swim-bladder is to the chub what the outer ear and the ear-drum are to us; as I said, a chub's ears are all inside. This may seem an odd arrangement, but a fish so equipped can hear sounds much as we can, as well as being able to feel the flow of water through its lateral line.

In fish as in men, the hearing organs depend on motion-detecting hair cells like those of the lateral line system. These hair cells can respond to movement of the fluid surrounding them, very sensitively, and in the inner ear they originally responded to the swirling of enclosed internal liquids so as to give a sense of balance and acceleration. When a sound wave reaches the inner ear, the molecules in the liquid move a little, to and fro, as the pressure rises and falls, and the hair cells in a specialised part of the inner ear detect these motions. All fish can hear a little with this sort of system; but fish with inner ears alone hear very poorly. The trouble is that sound waves pass through the fish, which after all is mostly water, much as they pass through water; that is, the rise and fall in pressure that constitutes the sound wave is transmitted well for a long way, but individual molecules of water move very little because water is nearly incompressible; and the inner ear hair cells detect movement, not changes in pressure. For sensitive hearing an animal needs a way of converting changes in pressure into fluid movement. The way that cyprinids and catfish do this is strikingly reminiscent of the mammalian hearing system; its efficiency may be one of the reasons why these are the most abundant of all freshwater fishes.

The human ear converts pressure to fluid movement by having the ear-drum between the outer ear, which concentrates sound waves, and the middle ear which is full of air; since air, unlike water, is very compressible the ear-drum can vibrate, moving in towards the middle ear as the pressure outside rises and out as it falls. This movement is transmitted across the middle ear by a chain of small bones slung from ligaments – again the bones are three in number, but this time they are modified jaw bones – and the last of these bones fits into a socket at the opening of the inner ear, so that when that bone moves it sets the fluids

The New Compleat Angler

Two cautious, lazy chub
below a bend in the still, hazy
heat of mid-summer

of the inner ear in motion, and specialised hair cells respond to the motion, and we hear sounds.

Now a fish, as I said, is made of almost incompressible tissues and swims in almost incompressible water; but its swim-bladder, if it has one, is full of compressible gases. So when a sound wave reaches it, the bladder will contract and expand as the pressure changes. The fish must feel this motion as the tissues around the bladder are pulled and pushed; if you have ever been in the deep end of a swimming pool as someone leaped from the high board, you will have felt the noise inside you as your diaphragm moved when the sound reached your lungs. Even this inner feeling is more efficient than the hearing of an unassisted inner ear; simply implanting an air-filled rubber balloon inside a flounder, which has no swim-bladder since it spends most of its time lying on the bottom and so has no need to float, is enough to improve its hearing threshold by ten decibels.

But in fish with Weberian ossicles the system is much more sophisticated. The swim-bladder has two walls, separated by oily connective tissue; the inner wall is complete and the outer has a lengthways slit, on the upper surface near the front. The edges of the slit are connected by elastic ligaments to the backbone, and the ligaments pull so as to keep the slit nearly closed. If the swim-bladder expands or contracts in response to sound, the slit widens or narrows as the well-lubricated surfaces of the outer wall slide over the inner wall. The edge of the slit is therefore the point where the greatest movement is produced by a pressure change; and it is from here that the chains of Weberian ossicles run, one from each side of the slit, forwards to liquid-filled canals in the skull which lead to the inner ears. The ossicles are slung from the backbone by ligaments shaped like leaf-springs, which help to swing them back as the bladder contracts.

So in these fish the swim-bladder acts as a sort of internal ear-drum, with the ossicles transmitting the movement to the inner ear. This is an excellent system, at its best low-frequency range as sensitive as a man's. The ossicles are essential; goldfish with their ossicles removed lose forty decibels sensitivity, an enormous drop. (To make a simple comparison; to make a sound decrease by forty decibels by moving away from it, in the open air, you must increase your distance nearly a hundredfold.) But much depends on the swim-bladder; the bigger the bladder, the greater the movement of the ossicles. Now the chub, being full of bones, needs a large bladder to compensate; the bladder is bigger in a chub than in another fish of the same size; no wonder, then, that the chub's hearing is so good.

There is one disadvantage in this cyprinid system of hearing, sensitive though it is. There is only one swim-bladder to detect the changes in pressure caused by the sound waves; so though there are two inner ears in the skull, it is hard to see how they can make out which direction any particular sound comes from, since the same bladder passes on the signals to both ears. Men, and all land vertebrates, have two completely separate ears, and can work out the position of a source of sound from the difference in its reception by the right and left ear. Fishes do seem able to find out such a position, but only by using their lateral line to detect the water displacement it causes (if it is close enough to them) or by swimming to and fro and hearing whether the sound gets weaker or louder.

This, from a fish's point of view (or hearing) is not too serious a drawback; especially in shallow and running water where sounds are very much scattered and absorbed and masked by other noises. Zoologists who have tried to train fish to respond to particular sounds have decided that a fish's hearing does not specialise in the same aspects of sound as a man's; a fish like a chub will hear sounds that a man would hear but will interpret them in a different way. When we listen, we analyse the wavelength of sounds – in musical terms, their pitch – very carefully; most people, without musical training, can tell the difference between two notes that differ in wavelength by half a per cent, and can distinguish between several notes played together. Our ability to sense where a sound comes from, too, depends on our perception that the pattern of sound waves analysed by one ear is slightly different from the other ear's; the ear nearer the sound detects the sounds slightly before the further ear, and from the difference one can work out the bearing of the source. But to analyse sound in this way one needs to listen to several waves of each sound as they pass. For an animal surrounded by air there is plenty of time to do this, especially if it is listening to high-frequency, short-wavelength sounds; many waves will reach its ear in a short time. Underwater, though, short-wavelength sounds, like short-wavelength light, are scattered and absorbed far worse than they are in air while long-wavelength sounds are transmitted fairly well, though not so far as in air; so fishes listen more to low, long-wave sounds, coming from fairly close. But they cannot afford to stay still and analyse several low-frequency, slowly-changing soundwaves coming from nearby sources which might be nearby enemies; if a fish in dark water starts to hear a sound of twenty cycles per second frequency, from an invisible source a few yards away, it dare not wait for even half a second to analyse ten wavelengths. Rather, it needs to be able to detect and respond to the sound very quickly, and to find out whether the sound is coming towards it or moving safely into the distance.

That is what the fish's inner ear does; no-one knows how exactly, no more than how the mammalian inner ear performs its prodigies of frequency analysis. Fish are not completely tone deaf; cyprinids can tell the difference between notes with frequencies 5 per cent apart; but they excel at responding rapidly to a brief sound that seems to get louder. Footfalls on the bank are just what is needed to set off a chub's alarm system. Some dedicated specimen hunters will put thick socks outside their boots to muffle their tread; every little helps. Those six small bones between the skull and bladder have led to a great deal of silent contemplation by careful anglers. One day it may be possible to attract fishes by the appropriate sounds; in Senegal the native fishermen make hollow lures which as the water flows through them produce a sound

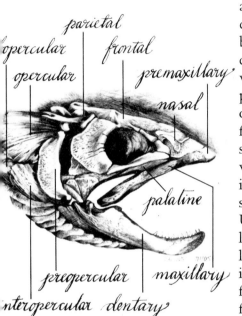

Major bones of the head

that is supposed to imitate the noise of a small fish feeding. And I once met a young man fishing (he said) for chub, from whose transistor a percussion band sounded at full volume. Perhaps he hoped to hypnotise them by repetitive drumbeats.

Even if you are totally silent you may alarm a chub by sight; its eyes are as good as a trout's, perhaps better for spotting anglers. The pupil, instead of being elongated forwards, is slightly distorted towards a triangular shape, one corner downwards and two up. This might improve its view of the bank. Chub have melancholy eyes, a gold circlet around the pupil set in a tarnished silver surround, with the greenish pigment that runs along their back and head coming down in dark loops around the sockets. A shy colouring generally, with orange-red tinges only in the tail and anal fins, not in the more prominent dorsal. Fortunately they often abandon their retiring moods and set out from their lurking holts, and can be tempted by carefully chosen baits even when cautious.

When they are not cautious, chub are quite omnivorous. The biggest chub ever caught in Britain, a ten-and-a-half pounder taken from the River Annan in 1955, later disqualified as a record fish on a technicality, fell to a fly fished as for trout; in fact, fished with the intention of catching a trout. Similarly, a good five-pound chub was once caught in Redmire Lake, on a floating crust intended for carp. In some trout rivers this inability to keep off other fishes' food has led to chub being persecuted, sometimes vilely; the practice of "fuddling skellies" was once common in the North and may not yet have vanished. Some chemists will supply *Cocculus indicus*, the ground dried fruit of *Anamirta cocculus*, the fishberry, a plant native to Malaya and the East Indies; this

A still-life of chub from the Stour, with quince from outside the studio and plover's eggs from an abandoned nest

A school of chub has a distinct feeding order. To hook the leader, usually the biggest, requires patience and precise observation. Time spent on reconnaissance . . .

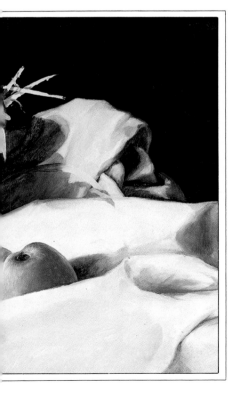

contains a powerful drug, picrotoxin. It is of little medical use; it has been tried as an antidote to barbiturate poisoning, and seems to be more used in South America than in Europe. Picrotoxin increases the rate of respiration, slows the heartbeat, and in large doses causes muscular convulsions; its great, non-medical virtue is that fishes are more sensitive to the poison than men are, and cyprinids are very sensitive even for fishes. The right dose of *Cocculus* in a trout stream will make any chub float to the surface, hardly able to move, while the trout are unharmed. But too much will wipe out all vertebrate life for some distance downstream. Far better than this sort of persecution is the enlightened practice of allowing selective fishing for chub in trout waters during the trout close season; for chub feed well in winter, and like most cyprinids they do not spawn till early summer. (As in other cyprinids, the males develop white spots over their heads before and during the spawning season, the "nuptial tubercules" which unlike the pimples of human adolescence seem attractive to females.)

Selective methods of taking chub are various. Most chub are probably taken on maggots and lobworms and bread-paste, unselectively, if some other fish does not gobble the bait first; cheese, as strongly flavoured as possible, is traditonally a good chub bait, nowadays supplemented by luncheon-meat. Some baits are excellent in

Chub rising with trout in a Cam mill-race. The chub is an unwanted intruder in a trout stream, although often of specimen size

the right season, when chub feed on one particular abundant food; caterpillars in summer, especially for chub lurking under an overhanging branch, or later in the year the fruit or berries of any tree that stands beside the water. (The trouble with tree-borne baits, though, is that it is often necessary to cast from the opposite bank from the tree beneath which the chub lies; this makes concealment more difficult.) In late summer and autumn, too, wasp grubs are very acceptable to chub, and half a dozen impaled on a large hook will often attract a good-sized fish. There are two difficulties with this technique; the first is getting the nest – if there is a local natural history society, it will probably contain a dedicated entomologist who can help you here – the second is using it for groundbait. Wasp nests are made from chewed wood, and float. If you throw fragments of the nest into a river they will drift uselessly away on the surface; if you put the nest into boiling water and break it up, then mix the waterlogged fragments with paste, the wasp-flavoured bait will sink attractively to the chub.

Grasshoppers I have already mentioned as a bait for dapping gently for chub. They are not so easy to catch as they were in Walton's day; not that they can jump further, but anglers nowadays rarely wear big broad-brimmed hats that they can scoop up insects in. Slugs are less agile, and nearly as good bait.

School of chub and a lone barbel above a drain paddle

Crayfish, too, make a very good and selective summer bait for large chub, though they are far better used to feed the angler. Lampreys are said to be almost too effective, for chub dash at them with great force. Being a fish used to rapid waters, with a long powerful body, the chub can move much faster than the average cyprinid, and though there is no difficulty in registering their bite at a lamprey the tackle may not survive.

The barbel, *Barbus barbus*, is the other big long powerful inedible cyprinid of British waters. Its shape is much like a chub's, but it is darker in colour and has a more flattened head; and its tail is curiously asymmetrical, with the lower lobe rounded but the upper lobe pointed. It is a bottom feeder, a river-pig, not at all fastidious; the big barbel of the Danube fall to worms taken from the Viennese sewers (but the worm must not be allowed to burst on the hook). Barbel nose into gravel and silt, and feel for food with the four long barbels, two on the chin and two at the angle of the underslung jaw; as well as feeling it they can sample its flavour, with the taste-buds on the barbels, before it enters their mouths. Sometimes they take food in midwater, conspicuously; they turn belly-upwards to get at it and the pale underside shows clearly. This turning over presumably lets them feel and taste the floating food, before swallowing it. It is obviously the beard-like barbels that give them their name; for "barb" meant "beard" in English, as it does in French, before it became restricted to pointed bits of metal. In the seventeenth century the two words were still interchangeable; if I may quote Dr Martin Lluelyn's *Song against Fishing* once more,

> *Break thy Rod about thy noddle,*
> *Keep thy Cork to stop thy bottle,*
> *Make straight thy hook, be not afeard*
> *To shave his beard,*
> *That in case of started stitches*
> *Hook and line may mend thy breeches.*

A barbel hooked

Some anglers may have been driven to follow this deplorable advice by the intolerable antics of barbel. They feed in shoals, indiscriminately and sometimes without fear, swimming even between the legs of those who would take them, and a lucky man with the right bait on the right day can go on hauling them in for ever. A Mr Warren, a perfumer by trade, on August 23rd 1771 caught two hundred and eighty pounds of barbel before noon at Waltham Deeps on the Thames; and stopped not because the fish were exhausted, but because he was. (There are hints by his envious contemporaries that his success owed something to secret

Ledgering for the small, powerful Lea barbel at King's Weir

perfumes in his bait.) At other times, barbel are preoccupied with small items of food that they grub up from the bottom, but if offered a small bait on a fine hook either ignore it or, worse, use their great strength to straighten out the hook or break the tackle. In the course of a year, more tackle probably gets smashed by barbel than by any other fish; people will try to take them as if they were roach, but barbel grow much bigger and are more powerful for their weight, and put up a fight worthy of any game fish. Some say that barbel can cut through the line with the thick sharp spine that forms the front of their dorsal fin; but this is probably an excuse, and the true blame should be given to inadequate lines.

The British rod-caught record is sixteen pounds one ounce, nearly four times the roach record; and there are some bigger than that, well over thirty pounds in European rivers. The closely related Aral barbel of the lower Volga and points eastwards grows to fifty pounds, and four feet. There are eight other smaller European species; and more in their Asian homeland. The great Indian barbel, the mahseer, is said to reach one hundred and fifty pounds. I don't know what sort of tackle it requires.

Even for English barbel you need a good Avon rod and strong wrists, and no end of groundbait, and a suitable river. Barbel prefer moderately fast, clean waters; the big ones often choose a region of slack water below a rapid run, with abundant cover; or they will lie in thick weed in the middle of a fast stretch. They are only worth fishing for in summer and autumn; in the cold weather, unlike chub, they go deep and become very sluggish, and then comes the close season.

It is usually said that barbel are native only to the east-coast rivers that once flowed into the Rhine, and have been introduced to western rivers only in the last century; but this is not certain. An Act for the better Regulation of Fisheries, from the time of Elizabeth I, imposes a fine of five shillings and confiscation of catch and tackle on anyone removing undersized salmon, trout or barbel from the Severn; an odd combination, surely, since barbel are poor food, but even odder if barbel were not then found in that river. An appreciation of the sporting qualities of inedible fish may go back further than one would have thought; though there is also a long tradition of confused lawmaking, usually to the benefit of the lawyers.

If a river contains barbel, they will eat almost anything on occasion; but specific, reliable baits are not always easy to find. Below weirs, barbel may be tempted by the silkweed that grows on the weir sill. A good standby is the clay ball full of worms, one of which is hooked; this immemorial technique contains all that is best in scientific groundbaiting, since it delivers attractive food (the worms, some of which will wriggle out of the ball) to a precise spot, and ensures that the bait can only be taken by the desired species (since only a big barbel will have the strength to break up the ball and remove the hook-bait). Such precision is clearly preferable to the simpler method of casting in a bucketful of bait by hand, with a hookbait in roughly the right place. This can ensure a concentration of groundbait around the hook only when fishing very close to the bank, which is probably not where the fish are.

For three centuries or more anglers have been trying to deliver other kinds of groundbait to a distance with the same accuracy as a ball of worms. The oldest form of bait dropper, perhaps, is the sheep's head or other inedible offal, hung from a branch to breed maggots that will bait the swim beneath for days. But this, too, only works fairly near the bank. In the late seventeenth century anglers around London, accustomed to the most heavily-fished coarse angling waters in the world, were experimenting with perforated tin boxes containing maggots or worms, which could be cast out into midstream to deliver groundbait to a selected region as the maggots crawled out. Mr Nicholas Cox, in *The Gentleman's Recreation* of 1674, gives a clear picture of such a device; not only is it more versatile than a clay ball, but a gentlemanly angler can use it and keep his fingers clean.

The modern plastic swimfeeder is a development of this, an aerodynamically shaped container that can be cast accurately for a long distance, and which releases maggots or other bait; a ledgered hookbait of the same kind is then positioned downstream of the swimfeeder. This elegant technique works well with most coarse fishes; barbel are perhaps the least suitable, for in their eagerness they often attack the swimfeeder. Some unscrupulous anglers therefore put hooks on the swimfeeder itself; I am not quite sure why I feel that this is cheating.

A caught barbel had better be returned to the river unless it seems a record. "A queasy meat and perilous for man's body," said Juliana Berners; I have found one recipe for cooking it, a Victorian one which despairingly suggests that it should be boiled with bacon and garnished with lemons, but I fear it would be a waste of bacon. Some parts may be better than others; Sir Epicure Mammon, anticipating the wealth that the philosopher's stone will bring him, drools in ecstasy:

> *My footboy shall eat pheasants, calvered salmons,*
> *Knots, godwits, lampreys: I myself will have*
> *The beards of barbels served instead of salads. . .*

but even Jonson doesn't make it sound too appealing. (Knots and godwits are small marsh birds; I have no idea whether they are in the same class as salmon and pheasant. We'll come to lampreys later.)

And if you must eat barbel, let it not be till well after spawning time. The roe can be alarmingly poisonous, and the rest of the fish may be tainted. Listen to the sufferings of Antonio Gazius, who in the sixteenth century took two mouthfuls of barbel roe in the interests of science:

> *At first I felt no inconvenience, but after some hours had elapsed I began to be disagreeably affected, and as my belly swelled, and could not be brought down by anise or other carminatives, I was soon in a state of great distress. An hour afterwards my countenance, as I have since been informed, changed and was pallid like that of a man in a swoon, and all the symptoms becoming rapid and more urgent, my friends were in the deepest anxiety. At length a deadly coldness crept over my body and limbs, and a violent flux ensued, from which, after vomiting and passing the offending pieces of roe, I ultimately recovered, though long labouring under such prostration of strength that my life was for some time judged in imminent peril.*

Gazius adds that the roe of pike is reputed by some to be similarly poisonous, but he understandably refrained from tasting it; as far as I know he was misinformed. Barbel roe may not always be as drastic a purgative as he reports; I shall suppress the name of the French physiologist who tested it on his own family and reported it ineffective; but I would prefer to learn from Gazius' experience rather than from my own.

RICHARD JONES' ROACH

Pikebait, Matchweight

Mustapha Kemal Ataturk, the victor of Gallipoli, father of modern Turkey and last of the benevolent despots, was once asked what quality he thought most important in a woman. He considered the matter, and from the wealth of his experience replied "Availability". The minor cyprinids – roach, rudd, gudgeon, dace, bleak, minnow – excel in this Turkish virtue; small and lacklustre they may appear in comparison with trout or carp, barbel or pike or salmon, but in the accessible lowland waters they are almost to be had for the asking; some of them may be taken in any water, at least in small numbers, without much effort. To the lordlier class of angler, such minor fish are only worth taking as bait for something much larger; to the naturally competitive who relish match-fishing, where the weight of the total catch is all that counts, they are the surest route to success. But many do not aspire to great pike, and find that the determined exertions of the match-fisher do not provide the quiet they seek. Listen to General Robert Venables, the first of many retired military men who have improved the tactics of angling, and whose *Experienced Angler* was often thought fit to be bound with Walton and Cotton's works: "In this pleasant and harmless Art of Angling a man hath none to quarrel with but himself, and we are usually so entirely our own friends, as not to retain an irreconcilable hatred against ourselves, but can in short time easily compose the enmity."

But Venables had no experience of a bank lined with determined matchmen, equipped with groundbait by the gallon and the intention to spoil the catch of their rivals downstream if they cannot do well themselves. Angling matches of a sort must be most ancient, even unscrupulous ones; Plutarch describes the famous contest between Antony and Cleopatra, where Antony hired a diver to place a great fish on his hook and Cleopatra, the next day, hired another to make him appear to catch a salted stockfish; but the concentration on weight of numbers is modern. Many who avoid the matchman's labours appreciate the attractions of angling for these minor cyprinids for relaxation: and some enter into the hunt for worthy specimens, and pursue angling records, finding as much effort and difficulty in the quest for a four-pound roach as for a fifty-pound carp.

The quest for a one-ounce minnow, come to that, must have its devotees; though the present British rod-caught record is only nine drachms, greater specimens surely exist. Minnows are the least of cyprinids; their name has affinities with *minimum*. *Phoxinus phoxinus*, the European minnow, is a pretty fish for its three inches, with a silvery belly that reddens in the spawning male, and a pattern of clearer blotches along the darker sides. It will slowly lighten or darken its colours to

A roach of two pounds would delight any angler: Richard Jones' record fish was over twice that weight

match its background; wise anglers wishing to use minnows as live-bait keep them in a white enamelled or plastic bowl, in which they become almost white and so show up better in the river. Walton, who on the testimony of his pupil Cotton was "the best hand in England with a minnow", his favourite bait for trout and coarser fish in the dark peaceful waters of the Thames and Lea, describes the elaborate fashion of his times by which he mounted a minnow on a single hook. His description reminds me of nothing so much as a devilish school exercise: take a class, all of whom know how to tie a shoe-lace, and get each to write down how to do so; then ask different pupils to follow each other's instructions to the letter; it is astonishing how few laces get.tied.

Somewhere there must have been an angling match that was won by a single minnow's weight; but the fish's great use has been as a laboratory species, far cheaper to feed and house than its larger cousins. Minnows, like the other cyprinids, are shoal fish. They swim in their native waters in great numbers – shoals of over five hundred minnows have been counted in the Thames – and the way that a shoal behaves, like a well-drilled, unanimous body, almost like a super-organism, is one of the wonders of the waters. Minnow shoals have been much studied, to find out how and why a hundred fish or more can move close-packed together.

"Why" is easier answered than "how". Minnows do not always shoal; in fairly gentle currents, and in safety, they form loose disordered groups in which each fish moves about independently, feeding on small fry and insects. But in swift-flowing water, or when threatened by a predator, they bunch together and form a shoal, with all fish moving together and in the same way. Minnow shoals are not exactly ordered; but on average each fish is nine tenths of a body length away from its nearest neighbour, with a tendency to be about 45 degrees away from due astern of the one in front, and a little higher or lower in the water than the ones beside it. Generally speaking, the members of a shoal of fish are all of about the same size; usually, all hatched in the same season; so if fish space themselves in terms of their own length the shoal will keep order, whatever the size of its members. (There are two consequences of the shoaling together of fish of the same age and size; first, since shoals of different sizes keep apart, if you are trying to catch a large specimen and you get several bites from a small shoal of the same species, you should go somewhere else unless you have reason to believe they will. Second, large old fish of whatever species tend to be solitary because all their former companions are dead.) Different species seem to have different preferred patterns; bream, for example, tend to form more regular shoals with each fish at right angles to its neighbour. The average spacing is always about one body length. The pattern is never regular and the shape of the shoal is always changing.

This shifting order has two advantages, it seems; one less certain than the other. It may be that each fish, except those in the front rank, can gain some advantage as it swims from the eddies in the water produced by the ones in front; much as each goose, in a V-shaped skein, gains lift from the eddies in the air produced by its predecessor. Some hydrodynamicists deny that this effect is important; others calculate that it may reduce the effort of swimming by as much as thirty per cent. If schooling does reduce the effort of swimming, it makes sense that minnows form schools in fast currents.

The other advantage is certain; fish in a school are less vulnerable to predators. All cyprinids, if threatened, bunch together, and the school they form carries out manoeuvres to baffle the enemy. If a pike or a perch approaches, the school will keep out of the danger zone in front of the predator's mouth; if it then moves to bring the school into its line of attack, the school will split into two groups, which swim to the left and right of the enemy and re-form behind his tail in safety. If the predator darts forward at the school, it explodes outwards in all directions, each small fish sprinting away from the point of impact so as to create an empty space into which the predator snaps. These escaping movements are astonishingly fast; I remember a winter day with a crust of drifted ice lying in a side-channel of the Stour, forming a layer thick enough to dampen out the wake of a mallard that swam past the ice's edge, and fry beneath it escaping upwards from a pike, so fast that they broke through the ice and lay thrashing on the surface, unable to return.

It seems that the multitude of quick movements confuses the predator, so that it cannot accurately fix the position of any one victim. Pike and perch in experimental tanks have shown that they can easily capture a solitary dace or bleak, have a little trouble with a small school of eight or ten, and perform much worse against twenty or more. It is not just that the predator cannot make up its mind which one to go for, since then there would be strong selection for a predator that chose one victim at random and set its course for that; rather, the predator cannot tell exactly where any one victim is or will be. There is an exact parallel here with various anti-aircraft systems, which have worked perfectly in peacetime trials when for reasons of economy they were given only one target at a time, but which when confronted with several hostile aircraft together work out the range of one, the height of another and the bearing of a third and infallibly miss all three.

This defensive schooling is of course more useful for prey species, which most cyprinids are, than for dominant predators; perch are unusual in forming aggressive schools. Some oceanic species like the tuna have been found to form schools that drive their prey into one

Shoaling bleak

killing ground. A hunting tuna school forms a parabolic curve, shaped like a cross-section through the reflector of a car's headlight. Just as light travelling in any direction from the headlight bulb to the reflector is sent forwards away from the reflecting surface in a parallel beam, so a parallel beam of light shining into the reflector would be concentrated at the position of the bulb; and so as a curved school of tuna swim forwards through the ocean, any other fish they encounter flee from the line of tuna and, wherever they meet the line, are driven to a central point which the school can eventually surround.

This must mean that the tuna have a remarkable ability to keep station; no-one knows how. Fish like minnows in simpler, densely-packed schools keep an approximate position through the operation of two senses together, sight and the lateral line. When shoals have been filmed changing course, and the slow action replay studied, it is seen that

A specimen rudd coming to the net . . .

each fish is responding to the average movements of many of its neighbours, paying more attention to the nearer ones. If the nerve to the lateral line is cut, a schooling fish can still keep station, though it will then swim directly abreast of its nearest neighbour and follow that neighbour only. A fish that is blinded (or in this humane age, fitted with opaque contact lenses) also keeps with the school, nearer to its neighbours than before. Deprived of both senses it will wander about helplessly.

It is probably because cyprinids must swim in schools that they have the sensitive neuromasts of their lateral lines enclosed in protective canals, under the skin and connected to the outside by a series of pores, even if they inhabit still water. Naked neuromasts like a pike's would be overwhelmed by the eddies from the rest of the shoal. And neuromasts inside a canal are only sensitive to movements in the water outside that set the liquid in the canal flowing. Delicate surgery can implant micro-electrodes in the nerve that leads to the lateral line neuromasts, and when this has been done (with roaches; minnows would need very delicate surgery indeed) the electrodes have recorded the nerves signalling in response to water flowing along the roach's side, from head to tail, but not to currents to which the roach is broadside on. So, a schooling cyprinid will be able to feel the eddies only from the fishes in front of it; and it seems to analyse these to work out what its neighbours as a whole

. . . and landed

are doing. But which fish takes the initiative in the manoeuvres of diversion and escape is uncertain.

The minnow's pre-eminence as a bait fish is due simply to its abundance; Nature has provided so many minnows as groundbait in so many streams. But there are waters where a better choice is the bleak, or blay, *Alburnus alburnus*, which is somewhat larger and very much more shiny; a slender, silver fish, but despite its pure colours much less choosy

than the minnow, which must have clear, clean water. The numbers of
bleak in the Thames at Oxford were much reduced after the municipal
reforms of the last century; vast shoals used to hang in the water below
the old sewer outfalls. In natural circumstances it feeds on water-fleas
and insects, and can be taken with fine artificial flies or with bluebottles
or maggots. It is an open-water fish, that avoids very overgrown or
silted places.

In 1680 one Monsieur Jacquin, cleaning the bleak he had caught in
the Seine (a very necessary operation, more so even than in nineteenth-
century Oxford) observed that the water he had washed them in looked
silvery, like pearls, with the tiny shining scales from the fish. His mind
turned to the profits to be made from artificial pearls; Italian wax
imitations, introduced to Paris some years before, had been
disappointing, tending to melt under the chandeliers of summer balls.
Thus was born the commercial bleak fishery, and the French artificial
pearl industry; for when the scales from the bellies of bleaks, the
silveriest of all, are washed clean of slime and ground up in water, they
form a paste which can be dissolved in liquid ammonia to form what the
French ingenuously call *essence d'orient*, a preparation which can coat
glass spheres to form lustrous pearls. M. Jacquin's first productions were
only partly successful, for the shining essence after a little while
transferred itself from the necklace to the neck; but he improved the
design and developed the first reliable artificial pearl, made from a
hollow glass sphere with the inner surface coated with bleak extract,
filled with white wax, and with the outer surface dulled a little to perfect
the deceit. Plastics have now replaced them, and protected the bleak;
though in the better quality Italian glass workshops the bleak essence is
still used for giving a surface iridescence, as of old, long-buried glass, to
modern antiquities.

These shiny scales give the bleak its name, for *blac* in Anglo-Saxon
meant, not black (which was, confusingly, *blaec*), but shining white;
hence *bleach* which whitens, and the *bleak* snow-covered winter
landscape, as well as the commonest of silvery fish. It is odd that this
Saxon name, now completely unintelligible without the aid of a

*Specimen-sized roach were
more common in Walton's day*

dictionary, should have stuck even though so many of the coarse fish have taken French names; gudgeon, roach, burbot, chevin, are all names that came over with the Norman conquest. That too is curious; it is well known that the names for meat (which the baron ate) are French – beef, pork, mutton – while the names of the living beasts (which the serf tended) are Saxon – ox, pig, sheep. Can it be that the Norman gentry had the leisure to go fishing while the serfs toiled, and gave French names to some of their catch, and ignored the small shining bleak? There was no match-fishing in those days; modern match-men cannot afford to neglect a species which can be locally most abundant, and the key to victory. The industrious Belgian angler Josef Isenbaert once took six hundred and fifty-two bleak from the Danube in a three-hour match, and well deserved his triumph; though some would consider such skilful exertion more like working on an assembly line than the contemplative man's recreation ought to be.

Though a school of bleak may appear to shine when seen from the bank, especially as they turn, such shining reflections are, underwater, a form of camouflage; for where all light is scattered and the view misty, a mirror that reflects the mist around it will at a short distance blend into the mist, whatever its colour. Fish scales reflect light because they contain enormous numbers of small thin flat shining crystals, about six million to the square inch. The crystals are of guanine, the nitrogenous compound that is a major component of guano, the fertiliser made from the droppings of fish-eating seabirds, and of a closely related chemical, hypoxanthine. They are cunningly arranged, so that the fish reflects light sideways but not upwards; they are stacked with their flat faces parallel so that light falling onto the faces will be well reflected, but light falling onto the side of the stack will pass through between the edges of the thin crystals; in the same way that a Venetian blind will let light pass through if the slats are edgeways on to the light. The stacks of crystals are aligned differently in different scales. On the side of the fish, they have their flat faces parallel to the surface of the skin, so that they reflect well sideways; but on the back, the stacks are set at an angle to the surface, so that they continue to reflect sideways but let light coming from above pass through. Occasionally a whole scale may become displaced; it will then look unusually dull, or unusually bright against its neighbours, depending on the angle of view.

Beneath the scales lie coloured pigment cells, usually greenish-brown on the back of freshwater fish; because of the alignment of the crystals in the scales, this colour can be seen when viewed from above, edgeways through the stacks of crystals, but not when viewed from the side. This is why most freshwater fish appear dark greenish-brown when viewed from above, though even the back looks shiny from the side. So even when near the surface a fish is concealed from above, as the top colouring blends with the dark water or bottom below, and also from the side, as it will reflect the scattered light coming from the water beside it. But if a fish rolls, it will reflect the daylight upwards from its shiny side, alerting the angler and perhaps signalling to other fish.

All that can be said about the gudgeon and the dace has been said before, about the barbel and chub, which are their larger cousins. The gudgeon, *Gobio gobio*, is a small, spineless barbel with only two barbels hanging from its lip, not four; with disproportionately large fins and a darker colouring, and a dark stripe along the lateral line. There is a possibly intermediate species, the Dalmatian barbelgudgeon, *Aulopyge hugeli*, which has the gudgeon's small size but four barbels; an odd fish, scaleless and with a wavy lateral line. (Anyone who plays the game of challenging others to build up complete words from their fragments will realise the potential of *Rbelgudg*.) No gudgeons grow to any size; six inches is big. They are bottom-feeders, easily taken with a worm or maggot, attracted by raking the bottom of a gravelly reach. They are attractive live-bait but often die quickly.

Roach in a junkshop window; the taxidermist's or the angler's art?

The dace is another matter; bigger than any gudgeon, and weight for weight as well-esteemed as chub or trout, except by narrow-minded persons who set out in pursuit of those species and cling to their specifications. John Dennys' angler had a nobler soul, who

> *. . . with watchful eye*
> *Attends the bite within the water clear*
> *And on the top thereof doth move his fly*
> *With skilful hand, as if he living were.*
> *Lo how the Chub, the Roach, the Dace and Trout*
> *To catch thereat do gaze and swim about.*

Lo how they do indeed, mutters the determined chub- or trout-hunter. The dace specialist has, of course, the opposite problem and quite a small chub would easily beat the dace record of one pound, four ounces, four drachms. They can be told apart; the dace is more silvery, has a smaller mouth and, decisively, has a concave outer edge to its anal fin; the chub's is convex. But there are eleven other species in the genus *Leuciscus*, as well as *L. cephalus* and *L. leuciscus* the dace; the orfe is the only other widespread one, and indeed six are restricted to Yugoslavia. An unscrupulous Croatian or Dalmatian angler could achieve miraculous record specimens.

Dennys' angler was unlucky to find roach, as well as the others, competing for his fly. Dace, like chub and trout, will cope with faster water than roach; and when they share the same stream, the dace feeds for choice in bright light, unlike other cyprinids. Any convenient fly for chub or trout will take dace if they are feeding; they are also very partial to the berries or caterpillars that fall from overhanging bushes. "A young dace is a bait for an old pike," said Falstaff: one of the few Shakespearean characters to show any practical knowledge of angling. (I hesitate to draw deductions from that last point.)

But it is not impossible that a roach should feed at midday; it is the most versatile of coarse fishes, the most common and widespread sizeable catch, the mainstay of many matches. *Rutilus rutilus* has been known as "an easy fish to catch" ever since the *Boke of St Albans* was written; they can be found abundantly in Britain, in most still waters or rivers that are not too fast, and for some reason the roach seem to grow bigger here than on the continent. "From British waters, records exist of roach about one kilogram in weight," says the admirable Danish ichthyologist B.J. Muus, with a touch of envy. Actually the biggest rod-caught roach came to four pounds one ounce; half that size would be a prodigy in many waters. Pessimists may explain the excellence of British roach by the absence of zander, which cannot last; optimists would attribute it rather to the skill of modern anglers, for a century ago (when there were no zander) a two-pound roach was thought as unlikely in Britain as a four-pounder today.

The biggest, best-fed roach are deep-bodied with a humped back; all young ones, and those in poorer waters, are as slender as a dace or chub. The eyes are reddish, and also the fins; the sides are silvery, sometimes bronzed, the back variously darkened. Roach love weeds, in which they find much of their food; leaves, larvae, shrimps, snails, anything. They do not much care what kind of plant; in the brackish Baltic they browse among bladderwrack, and in former times some of the best roach fishing was to be had beside wooden ships returned from the tropics, moored in the Thames or Bristol Avon with a thick trailing undergrowth. If there are no weeds about they prefer a hard to a muddy bottom.

Omnivorous roach may be tempted by any small bait: maggots that resemble the larvae on which they usually browse, worms, bread paste or flakes, caddis larvae, hempseed. There are innumerable recipes for improving the appearance or flavour of the bait, all earnestly believed in by their practitioners; few nowadays as complex as the "alluring ointments" of the seventeenth century. Walton mentions some of the more reputable of them, made from turpentine and honey and distilled oak-gall, or ivy-gum and spikenard, or the marrow of a heron's thighbone. James Chetham, of Smedley near Manchester, his younger contemporary, believed in more necromantic mixtures; his *Angler's Vademecum* of 1681 gives recipes for anointing the eight inches of line next the hook, for which "some have such confidence, that they affirm they'll not only allure, but even compel Fish to bite . . . highly commmended by Monsieur Charras, Operator and Apothecary Royal to the present French King, Lewis the Fourteenth." Man's fat (to be had from any dissecting-room), cat's fat, powdered Egyptian mummy, camphor, Venice turpentine, cumin seed and civet were the main ingredients; there are simpler ways of making a greased line float. Alternatively, says Chetham, "Take the Bones or Scull of a dead Man, at the opening of a Grave, and beat the same into powder, and put of this powder into the Moss wherein you keep your worms."

Roach on the River Lark

ROACH ON THE LARK

Flavouring the bait is to the modern mind more logical than flavouring the line; but what should we make of Meister Johan Adam of Frankfurt, who a century earlier had recommended anglers to anoint their hands with a mixture of pounded snails, ammoniacal salt, glow-worms and honey? "Rub thy hands and thou shalt see wonders," he said; perhaps the glow-worm extract shone in the dark.

The roach remains a favourite quarry of the freshwater angler

There may be something in some of the flavouring recipes (I know of no-one who has tried Chetham's, or Adam's), for roach like all cyprinids have a very sensitive sense of smell. Schools of cyprinids are held together partly by their smell; any cyprinid placed in a tank will swim towards an inlet from which water flows from another tank containing other fish of the same species. (But the sense of smell cannot give very precise information about the position of other members of the school, and is of little help in keeping station.) And von Frisch, the perceptive biologist who also discovered the food-signalling dance of bees, found that an injured cyprinid gives out a different smell, an alarm substance which will cause a shoal of that species to break up as its members flee, as if from an attack, even if they can see no predator nor the injured victim. Likewise, fish can detect the smell of their enemies; dace placed in water in which a pike has been kept are thrown into panic, leaping out of the water to escape their unseen enemy. Therefore it is most important not to touch your bait with fingers that have just handled an injured fish, or a pike or perch. Some purists go so far as to rub their hands in the mud of the bottom to be sure of disguising any foreign flavour before they touch the bait.

It appears that most of these flocking and alarming odours are produced by fairly small molecules, peptides and amino-acids, which are readily available or could be made synthetically. (Perhaps it is only coincidence that such molecules, which are produced when proteins break down, must have been present in Chetham's nauseous pastes.)

This knowledge opens the way to really scientific swimfeeding, with flavours that will attract shoals of roach (or still better, bream); or in a match in which the man downstream is attracting all the fish of one species, an alarm signal to disrupt his shoal but not your own. In some fishes the communication by smell is even more complex; among the American ictalurid catfishes, each fish has an odour which informs others of its position in the local hierarchy. The smell of a large, dominant fish is enough to send lesser catfish into hiding; and the underlings can perceive any loss of status by their superior. If a big catfish, the undisputed champion of a fish-tank, is taken to another tank where an even bigger and more powerful fish subdues him, on his return

Walton says that an otter can smell a fish a hundred yards away. The Chinese fish with them in the same way that we use dogs to retrieve hares

he no longer exudes dominance; his smell will not terrify his former subordinates, who will for some time stand up to him.

This raises the still more elegant possibility of a small bait reeking of dominance, which would selectively draw forth the biggest fish in the water to do battle; but I do not know whether it would work for other fish besides ictalurids. And American fishermen have a very effective, unchivalrous scent-lure for ictalurids as it is; they put one female in a trap in the spawning season and take all her suitors.

Failing such miraculous baits, a roach may be taken in a manner that has not changed in essentials since the sixteenth century. John Dennys' *Secrets of Angling* contains the elements of one style:

> *There see on yonder side where one doth sit*
> *With Line well twisted, and his Hook but small;*
> *His Cork not big, his Plummets round and fit,*
> *His bait of finest paste, a little ball*
> *Wherewith he doth entice unto the bit*
> *The careless Roach, that soon is caught withall:*
> *Within a foot the same doth reach the ground,*
> *And with least touch the float straight sinketh down.*

Well-twisted line is no longer a problem, as we do not have to rely on horse-hair; the small hook, small bait set to swim at the right depth and the delicately-balanced float are essential. For the roach, careless though it is, a water-sheep to the barbel's water-pig, bites or rather nibbles gently and is to be taken with fine, very sensitive tackle, as delicate as the stream will allow; with the line as straight as possible, so as to allow a rapid strike the moment a bite is registered. Apart from the speed of the strike and the observation of the slightest movement of the float, the skill lies in presenting the bait; "laying-on", holding the float stationary

To die in poisoned sludge is an unworthy end

against the current so as to allow the bait to lie on the bottom, temptingly near a weed-bed; "swimming the stream" or, with heavier end-tackle and more skill (or confidence) "long-trotting", drifting the bait in front of the float downstream to search out a length of water; "tripping", with the float set higher so that the bait moves over the bottom. Dennys' angler was presumably swimming the stream; it is probable that he would not have heard of the modern improvement of fishing "on the drop", in which the drifting float is gently checked so as to let the bait swing upwards, and then drop completely naturally, in free fall unrestrained by the line, as the float is released. This is a killing method and is not mentioned in print till this century; how long it may have been practised by illiterate, or secretive, anglers is unanswerable.

But as well as innovations, roach-fishing especially has very old techniques. It is only in angling for roach, or bleak, that the long reelless rod, the roach-pole, is still preferred to the reel and shorter rod; it allows more accurate placing of the bait than most people can achieve by casting, and astonishingly swift striking and hauling in of the fish. Eighteen to twenty feet is a good length for a cane roach-pole; recently, the ten-meter carbon-fibre pole has been produced, and who knows what wonders it may not perform? Old techniques and ultra-modern equipment are a striking combination indeed. Playing a big fish on a long pole has its difficulties, though; unscrewing the bottom joints is strongly recommended.

Walton memorably defines the rudd as "a bastard small roach"; the confusion is understandable, and continues. Usually the rudd, which has a very patchy distribution, mostly in still waters, is taken for the roach which is almost ubiquitous in the lowlands. In fact the rudd is not one of the eight European species of *Rutilius*, but is in a genus by itself, *Scardinius erythrophtalmus*; though the "red-eye" which is the meaning of its species name proclaims its similarity in appearance to the roach. Both have deepened bodies and red-tipped fins; the differences are slight but unmistakable. The rudd, much more of a surface feeder than the roach, has an up-turned mouth with a protruding lower lip, so that it can easily take food from below; its body behind the pelvic fins forms a sharp keel; and, most distinctively, the rudd's pelvic fins lie in front of a line dropped from the dorsal fin, while the roach's lie directly below it. The Irish simplify matters, after their fashion, by having no roach (except for a few local introductions) and plentiful rudd, which they call roach.

To complicate things further, rudd interbreed rather frequently with other cyprinids; sterile hybrids with roach, bream and silver bream have all been recorded. Bleak/chub, bleak/roach, bleak/bream, roach/bream, roach/silver bream, and bream/silver bream crosses are also known; all cyprinids that spawn at about the same time, in early summer over weed-beds, with vast excitement; some anglers claim to have heard a hissing noise made by multitudes of spawning fish rubbing together, and to have seen the smaller fish lifted bodily out of the water by the pressure of the throng. But the rudd seems to be more often indiscriminately promiscuous than others. And a rudd/roach hybrid is remarkably like both its parents; worse, from a specimen-hunter's point of view, a rudd/bream hybrid looks very like an exceptionally large rudd. Fortunately, the number of rays in the anal fin differs; nineteen to twenty-three in bream, fifteen to eighteen in bream/rudd (brudd?), ten to thirteen in rudd. Otherwise, cyprinid hybrids can be reliably distinguished by the shape of their teeth, but this calls for dissection. For all cyprinids are "leather-mouthed fishes", with no visible teeth in their mouths but with hidden teeth in their throat, one to three rows, distinctively shaped, mounted on the pharyngeal bones behind the last gill-arches. These pharyngeal teeth can cut or crush the food, against a horny plate set in the roof of the throat, as it passes down; the rudd's have characteristic serrated edges. To a real anatomist, these are the fundamental structures for cyprinid classification; unfortunately, you have to kill and cut up the fish to get at them.

The true rudd, where it exists (the best are in the Norfolk broads and the Irish loughs) love shallow, sheltered still water. They can be fished for as if they were roach, but with this added difficulty, that the copious ground-baiting that roach-fishers indulge in will, in rudd waters, very likely attract fish-scaring waterfowl before the fish. Fly-fishing is more often employed for the surface-feeding rudd than for the roach; adding a maggot to the fly is not considered unsporting. Very recently it has been discovered that roach, and probably all cyprinids, have an unexpectedly complex kind of colour vision; as well as the porphyropsin-based red receptor cells in the retina, which one would expect in a red-finned, dark-water fish, and green- and yellow-sensitive cells too, they have a short-wave violet-sensitive set of receptors quite unlike anything in other fish. It is not at all clear why they specialise in seeing violet, or what the world looks like to a fish with four-colour vision; but there may be scope for special violet-patterned, cyprinid-selective flies that might be inconspicuous to trout.

Actually, though, the rudd do not care too much what a bait, real or artificial, looks like; they can be taken on bare, shining golden hooks; without the excuse of the equally undiscriminating mackerel which cannot slow down to examine its food because it breathes on the ramjet principle, and suffocates if it stops moving. The rudd's virtue is that it is far less deterred by heat or bright light than the roach, or most other fish, and can give entertaining sport in pleasant weather. In the warm springs of Baile Epicopesti in Rumania there are rudd that are acclimatised even to water at 34°C, near blood heat; but they are stunted and short-lived, not worth travelling to fish for.

Idle Longevity

The three big cyprinids, the bream and the tench and the carp itself, are well worth the journey to the still or slow waters where they lurk; big, browsing, idle, slow-moving, stately long-lived fish. Big enough to be worth some care in cooking: hungry men have eaten roach, and for all I know minnows, but there are better sauces than hunger for a carp. Big enough, too, to attract giant-killing anglers; and big enough, in a fishing match, to outweigh shoals of lesser fish.

Actually only the bream, *Abramis brama*, is a reliable matchwinner; tench or carp are unlikely to be found away from cover with a multitude of anglers about. And perhaps "reliable" is not the right word. Bream feed in shoals that move along favourite tracks that are well-defined but, to most humans, unpredictable; a matchman who finds that a bream shoal has chosen the water near his peg is in luck, but if they decide to feed elsewhere there is little he can do but grumble about fish that turn a match from an exercise of skill to a form of angling bingo. Unless, indeed, the bream take up station shortly downstream of his pitch; he can then cast in bream groundbait by the bucketful in the hope of filling their guts and diverting them from his neighbour's hook, getting them to move further out than anyone can fish, and perhaps luring them upstream a little. Nearly all is fair in match-fishing; not quite all. I suppress the name of the Belgian angler who, under pretence of removing the hooks, shoved lead wire down his captives' throats; to judge by what they do with racing yachts, the French will soon go one better and use depleted uranium.

The bream is mostly a bottom feeder that sucks up mud and food together into its mouth, and spits out the mud. The mouth has a system of sliding, multiply-hinged jaws that allow it to form a protruding tube, to penetrate the bottom better; as they feed, bream hover nearly at right angles to the bottom, sucking up and blowing down, to clear away the mud around some interesting morsel. At night they come right up to the margin to feed thus, leaving a series of characteristic "bream pits" up to four inches wide which can be clearly seen in the shallows; the darkness protects them, for they must swim with their tails at the surface when they make the pits, and in daylight would surely attract predators.

In the daytime they move away from the bank into deeper midstream waters, where they are safe from herons and less conspicuous to anglers. They can still be detected by the experienced eye; sometimes as they feed they send up small clouds of muddier water from the bottom, forming a darker patch where the shoal feeds. Often, the mud is saturated with gases produced by the rotting vegetation buried in it; as the bream suck up the mud, they release the gas, which escapes from

The slow-moving, muscular and sedate tench, a most powerful and demanding adversary

their gills as strings of bubbles, about the size of peas, which also betray their presence. (These gases must be largely methane, which is inflammable; a pyromaniac friend once suggested a scheme for causing electric sparks just above the water surface, which would ignite the methane and cause a sort of will-of-the-wisp glow so that the shoal could be seen from a great way off. There are, fortunately, technical difficulties which have so far deterred him.) And at some times the bream swim close to the surface and roll, smoothly but shiningly, causing little disturbance in the water but showing their broad silver sides. It is this bright sporting near the surface that gave the bream its name, long ago; from an old Teutonic root that must have been something like "breswan", meaning to glitter.

The bream's shape seems designed to cause the greatest possible reflection. It has the deepest, thinnest body of any cyprinid; should it decide to lie on its side, it would make a very passable flatfish. At its greatest depth, from the hump in front of the dorsal fin down to the pelvic fins, it can measure more than a third of its length. And only the strip along the back is darkened; the flanks are greenish-silver when young, more brassy in older fish but still bright.

This shape has two advantages and one disadvantage. A fish that stands on its head in shallow water needs as short a body as its size will permit. A long, powerful tail like a trout's or a barbel's is of no use if it waves in the air. Bream, in fact, swim more with their bodies and their anal fin than with their rear portions; amputating the tail fins reduces the thrust by only forty-five per cent, so even if the tail does break the surface relatively little power will be lost. And a short, deep, flat body is excellent for a fish that relies for concealment on the principles of mirror camouflage that our architects are now starting to use for office blocks. The flattened shape ensures that as much of the fish as possible reflects light sideways, where it will blend into the scattered background light, and as little as possible is visible from above or below. For a fish cannot reflect light upwards if it is to remain unseen from above; it can at best only have a darkened upper surface that will blend more or less with the darkness below, but for a fish near the surface or in shallow water this gives imperfect camouflage. And when seen from below (a favourite angle of attack for predators like pike or otters, that look forwards and upwards for choice) any fish, no matter how bright its belly, must appear dark and conspicuous against the sky. From either of these two vulnerable directions the flattened bream, seen edge-on, is less obvious than a round-bodied fish would be. And the bream's depth of body probably confers some immunity from attack by pike and zander.

The disadvantage is that when swimming forwards this short, deep body produces much less thrust, and more drag, than a rounder, more streamlined body of the same weight. But then, bream avoid strong currents and do not need to exert themselves. Consequently, they show little fight when hooked; the story is well known, of the angler who thought he had caught a lily-leaf and found it was a six-pound bream. Even bigger ones (the British rod-caught record is thirteen pounds nine ounces, but they come much bigger in the great lakes of Eastern Europe) produce little struggle when caught. To the matchman, of course, the bream's lack of sporting qualities is a blessing; the last thing he wants is an exciting, long-drawn-out fight; far better to have a big fish that can be hauled in like a wet rag, into the keepnet at once, and another as soon as possible. The only time a bream can give serious resistance is if the angler strikes too hard when the fish is at a wide angle to his line; the resistance of a big bream being jerked sideways through the water is more than it can ever achieve by swimming forwards.

Detecting the bite, and timing the strike, are the difficult part of bream fishing. For such a bottom feeder, almost all baits are legered on the bottom; though a few big predatory bream have been taken by spun minnows, or by surface flies on a hot day. Bread, worms and freshwater mussels attract them well, and maggots in roach waters where they have acquired that taste from copious groundbaiting. The problem is that bream, in their normal feeding, suck up their food gently and spit it out, perhaps several times, to clean it before swallowing it. To perceive the slight movement of the bait as the fish begins its exploration, the traditional method is to rig a float that will tip over as the weight of the bait, and the shot beside it, is lifted by the bream; some keen-eyed experts, on a calm day in still water, can manage without any float, and observe only the movement of a slightly slackened line. The Great Modern Improvement is the swing-tip, an additional length of rod attached to the end of the top section by a flexible tube, with runners to carry the line through it. With the swing-tip placed low down, close to the water, and the line tightened, the slightest movement is easily seen. Modern is a relative term; the swing-tip mounted on rubber or plastic tubing dates back to the fifties, but its ancestry is much older. In 1805 the *Elastic or New Invented Superficial Float* was described, though its inventor was not named; an ordinary quill float, but attached to the tip of the rod by five or six pig's bristles, twisted and wound with fine waxed silk thread, to give a flexible joint. The line was passed through the runners on the rod, and through the loops on the float, and then: "when you want to fish, let your line sink gently: you will feel when the shot touches the bottom, as it will give your float a visible check; then raise your line a little . . . when you have a bite, this float will have the same motion as the common float, although out of the water.

"Among the many advantages this new float has above the common one, are these. Your float will never frighten the fish; small fish will never play with it; nor will it disturb the water . . . among weeds you will find it answers beyond your expectation. When you strike, the rod, line and fish has but one motion; but with the common float there is three if your line is long; the first motion is your rod, second your line, and third the float and fish, if the first motion has not frightened him away: but with this New Elastic Float, your line is infallibly perpendicular from the tip of your line to the bait, and of course there can be but one motion when you strike, as the float is no impediment . . . No float can equal this for Roach angling."

Overleaf
A school of bream feeding by the margins in late July; some, over ten pounds, lurk in deeper water

SHOAL

Such an indicator is excellent for bream too. It seems that pigs' bristles lack the real elasticity of rubber tubing, for the great sensitivity of the swing-tip is not mentioned among the Elasticated Float's virtues. But rubber then was soft and sticky, and nearly melted in summer sunlight; the vulcanisation process, in which the gum is treated with sulphur and becomes harder and more heat-resistant, was not invented till later in the nineteenth century, after the first rubber-soled shoes had entrapped their wearers in summer. The use of a swing-tip as an indicator of delicate bites, then, may be said to be truly modern; as is the use of wind-shields, mounted beside the rod-tip to stop the breezes registering as bites.

As well as the common (or bronze) bream, there are also Pomeranian and silver breams, that may be taken in much the same way. The former is in fact a bream/roach hybrid, intermediate in shape and size between its parents; with whitish fins unlike the red-finned roach, without the bream's long distinctive anal fin – the Pomeranian's has only twelve to fourteen rays, as against twenty-three to thirty-one in the true bream – and with a roach's symmetrical tail-fins, unlike the bream which has a longer, more rounded lower lobe. The silver or, more disparagingly, tinplate bream, *Blicca bjoernka*, is a separate species; less closely related to the common bream than some of the Continental cyprinids, the Danube bream *Abramis sapa* and the zope *A. ballerus*, but outwardly similar. Silver bream are smaller (a pound is a good average size, four and a half the record), and even when old still silvery; their paired fins have a reddish tinge near the base, and pale grey tips, while the common bream's are darker. The really distinguishing feature, as is often the case for cyprinids, is the pharyngeal teeth; all *Abramis* have one row, *Blicca* have two. Since the only worthwhile feature of the common bream is its size, it is hard to get excited about smaller varieties.

There are many excellent recipes for cooking delicious bream, but unfortunately they all refer to the sea-bream; spiny-finned fishes with the same deep body, but with firm reddish tasty flesh and excellent sporting qualities; not the same fish at all. *Abramis brama* needs careful handling but can be made quite tasty, to those who do not have a prejudiced palate that despises coarse fish. Let such persons be grateful that they do not live in the past times of compulsory fish-eating, when they might have suffered like Monsieur Claude Guillon, beheaded at Sainte Claude in Burgundy in 1627 for eating meat on a Friday; horsemeat, at that.

In Russia, where coarse fish grow to monstrous sizes and the sea is far away, they understand the art of cooking cyprinids with sweet-sour sauce; one of the many qualities they will not thank you for telling them they share with the Chinese. Bream cooked with wine, peppercorns and sultanas in the Russian manner acquires a reasonable taste; boiled in lightly salted water, after the English style, its flavour matches its fighting qualities. Here is the Russian recipe: simmer a chopped onion, leek, carrot and stick of celery for a quarter of an hour in a saucepan with three-quarters of a pint of water; add a quarter of a pint of dry white wine, a dozen peppercorns, an ounce of sultanas, a little parsley, a bay leaf, two tablespoons of vinegar and one of lemon-juice; and (if you have no better fish to cook) two pounds of filleted, de-scaled bream. Simmer for another twenty minutes. Then melt in a small pan an ounce of butter and stir in a tablespoon of flour, over a low heat, till smooth. Remove the fish, strain the stock it has cooked in, and stir half a pint of the stock to make a sauce with the flour and butter; add a teaspoon of white sugar to the sauce, cook for a few minutes, add another half-ounce of sultanas and pour over the bream.

I forgot to say what no-one who has handled a bream will dispute, that it has a liberal coating of slime. This protects it from parasites; some hydrodynamicists hold that the friction-reducing slime reduces drag and lets fish swim faster through the water, but this can hardly be a matter of importance for bream. The tench, *Tinca tinca*, is exceptionally slimy even for a fish: and there are no end of fables about the medicinal virtues of its slime; of how injured pike will heal themselves by rubbing their wound against a tench's side; of how pike recognise their physician and will not attack it; of headaches cured by laying a tench across the temples, jaundice cured by laying it across the belly, and Rondeletius' sadly imprecise account, relayed by Walton, of "a great cure done by applying a tench to the feet of a very sick man . . . done after an unusual manner, by a certain Jew."

A great secret, on which the reputations of many doctors and saints are founded, is that most people recover, more or less, from most diseases, at least for a while; and whatever treatment or prayers precede the recovery gain the credit. This seems to be the reason for the reputation of the tench; at least, it can have done no harm. Some authors recommend a similar cure for headache, but with an electric ray instead; I would not be so certain that this primitive form of shock therapy was harmless. It is true that no-one has definitely proved that tench slime has no beneficial activity; but then Pliny (father of lies, *et cetera*) says that diamonds dissolve in goat's blood, and no-one ever got a research grant to investigate that either.

As for the grateful avoidance of tench by pike, the sad truth is that pike will go for anything that moves within range of their jaws, if it is not too big or too fast. But truth is as strange as fiction; there are coral reef fishes, the cleaner wrasses, which assist much larger fish, cleaning their teeth and gills and removing parasites. The larger species do not attack the wrasses, but perform a sort of head-downwards fin-waving dance to solicit their attention. Skin-divers have reported unsolicited wrasses removing the scabs from cuts on their arms and legs; a doubtful benefit.

The kernel of truth in the fable is that other fish do rub themselves against tench, no-one knows why, and tench are rarely taken by pike; but that is due to the difficulty of finding, and catching them. For tench are very much weed-haunting fishes, drably camouflaged; quite unmistakable when seen out of water, nearly invisible in it. The heavily-built body, thickset right back to the tailfin, is olive-green or darker, sometimes a brown that is nearly black; in ornamental tench, golden orange; with dark fins, orange-red eyes, and unusually for a cyprinid a multitude of small scales rather than big shining plates. The scales have a subdued bronze lustre on the flanks, and a darker red-gold tinge on the belly. In some big old tenches the belly is redder, even vermilion. This was the case with the famous tench of Thornville Royal in Northamptonshire, whose capture Daniel describes; when the moat beside the manor house was drained in November 1801, they found some four hundred believable tench and, hidden among the roots of a tree, what they at first took for an otter; a great tench two feet nine inches long, Daniel says, and eleven pounds nine and a half ounces. Something must be wrong here; for the weight (not much greater than the modern rod-caught record of nine pounds ten ounces, less than the twelve pounds eight ounces of one netted in the Kennet in 1951) is far too light for the length. Optimists may hold that scales, in 1801, were far more likely to be misleading than measuring-rods; pessimists may notice that some of Daniel's other stories are patently unworthy of a gentleman in holy orders - notably the one about live pike being exposed by fishmongers with their breasts cut open, to show how fat they were, and the wounds of those unsold being healed by the application of a tench's slime.

The tench is the only British freshwater fish in which the sexes can be easily distinguished, apart from the breeding livery; the males have longer pelvic fins that reach back to the vent, and the second ray of these fins is markedly different. These differences appear when tench are in their second summer, about six inches long; in the third or fourth year they start to spawn. The breeding season stretches unusually late into summer, from May to August or even September; nevertheless tench-fishing starts at the end of the usual coarse close season, in June. This is unkind but essential, for tench are extraordinarily sensitive to changes in temperature; about 68°F is reported to be the optimum feeding temperature, but a few degrees warmer is too much for them, and with the first cold nights of autumn, generally by the end of September, they bury themselves in the mud and go into a long torpid hibernation.

To balance this sensitivity to temperature, they are not over-sensitive to anglers. Loud noises will alarm them, like any cyprinid, and they intensely dislike bright light; but they can be approached from a boat much more easily than a bream or carp, and seem to be actually attracted by dragging or raking the bottom. And their eyesight is poor; a much thicker line can be used for a tench than for a bream.

This last is convenient, for though tench-fishing much resembles bream-fishing in technique, there are two important differences. A tench will take the same baits as bream, and likewise stands on its head to feed so that the bite is registered by the lift of the float as the bait is raised; it also feeds by sucking mud into its mouth, though the bubbles it sends up are very numerous and very small, no bigger than pinheads, and it rarely creates a perceptible cloud of mud. Usually the bubbles are a sign that it is digging for bloodworms, and then an oxblood bait, or one of the

Specimen bream for the table

modern high–protein fishfoods, is the least ineffective. Those who despair of getting tench to bite on warm evenings, otherwise suitable, when the fish have decided to go off their food can always try Walton's recipe of flavouring the bait with tar, or Dame Juliana's of toasted brown bread with honey. If either writer is to be trusted, I would back the Abbess.

The differences are that the tench will always be near a mass of horrible entangling weed – dedicated tenchmen spend the last days of the close season cutting a clear pathway to the bank, out of which the tench flees at the first sign of trouble – and that it has an unexpectedly powerful pull. A contented tench ambles along, taking its time, feeling the bottom with its two short barbels, rowing itself with its paired fins and gently backing water with a sort of underarm-bowling movement. But when it feels itself in danger, it is surprising what force the rounded body and thick muscular tail will produce. A line of six pounds breaking strain would be excessive for bream, quite realistic for tench; and if a big tench gets well into the weed and submerged roots, six pounds breaking strain won't help.

Mr Richard Walker has an explanation for some disasters that occur even before the tench reaches the undergrowth. In his experience, some big tench wait for several seconds, still idle, after feeling the hook, and then make their powerful dash for cover. If this dash coincides with the angler's decision to haul in the small fish he thinks he's hooked, then farewell tench and farewell tackle. Whether they do it out of malice is not certain.

When you have caught a tench you will do better to cook it than to use it for medicine. Tench, like carp, are less favoured in the kitchen than they once were; before rapid transport and refrigeration were available, there was a great deal to be said for fish that could survive for hours or days out of water, carried to market in great creaking waggons on beds of moss or straw sprinkled with water to keep them moist, nourished on bread sopped in milk, or in emergencies brandy. In the middle ages, and till much later in Catholic countries, no substantial house was complete without its ponds of big cyprinids, and especially the stew-ponds of clean running water to keep the fish in for a few days before they were killed, to cleanse them of the muddy taste of stagnant waters. This last refinement is not so necessary for tench as for the deeper-rooting carp and bream, and for river-caught tench can fortunately be dispensed with.

The quickest way to cook tench is to scale and clean them and fry them or bake them, in a fairly hot oven, in rather a lot of butter, for about fifteen minutes for a two-pound fish. This simple recipe is greatly improved by lining the buttered baking-dish with a layer of chopped onions, with seasoning of salt, pepper and parsley according to taste; lay the fish on the onions, coat with melted butter, put in the oven and when nearly cooked add a couple of glasses of dry white wine, baste it thoroughly, add a quarter of a pint of cream with a squeeze of lemon and bake for five minutes more.

Or, more sumptuously, the tench can go with other river fish into a *matelote*, that nourishing French fish stew which Brillat-Savarin, the Philosopher of the Kitchen, said had unsurpassable virtues, notably that one can go on eating it almost indefinitely without feeling full or fearing indigestion. I have never been able to test his assertion; the dish is, as he said, brought to perfection in riverside inns, but since his day the French inkeeper's attitude to guests who want to go on eating stew indefinitely has become less sympathetic.

To make a *matelote* you need an eel and another, less oily fish; a tench or a carp or ideally both. Clean the eel, cut off its head and cut it into slices about an inch thick; clean and scale the other fish, cut off their heads and fins, and slice them too. Melt an ounce of butter for each pound of fish in a deep pan. For each ounce add a couple of small onions, chopped. Brown the onions gently, then add a tablespoon of flour for each ounce of butter and stir till smooth. Then add a clove of garlic, salt and pepper, and the best part of a bottle of robust red wine. (No nonsense about white wine for fish; a *matelote* without eel and red wine is worthless.) Simmer for about ten minutes, then add the fish slices, rolled in flour; cook with rather more heat for another twenty minutes, by which time the sauce should be quite creamy. Some people add a glass of cooking brandy a few minutes after adding the fish, and set light to it; I am not sure how this improves the sauce, but it is the best fate for some brandies. If, when you clean the tench, you find the roes still full, you

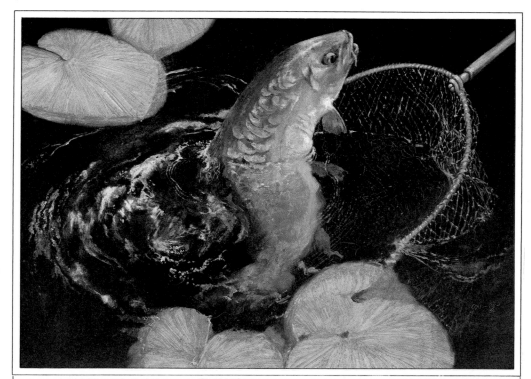

Mirror carp netted (above) and another landed at night. There are carp fishermen, and others for whom angling is only a sport

can boil them, cut them into pieces, dip them in batter and fry them as an accompaniment to the stew; which goes well with toast or fried bread.

But no matter how fine a *matelote* or any other fish dish may be, there are some anglers who would never consent to waste a sizeable carp in mere cookery. To the serious carp fancier, it is obvious that anyone who succeeds in landing such a noble fish should handle it reverently, weigh it, measure it and then return it to the water, to grow larger and warier still. Carp worship is an oddly distributed religion, found erratically across Europe and Asia, most intense in the offshore islands at each extremity, Britain and Japan. The Japanese admire the carp's enduring courage, and the way it submits decorously to its fate on the chopping board, and venerate its longevity. The fifth of May is the Boy's Carp Festival, *Koi Noburi*, when everywhere great paper carps are flown as kites, or rather windsocks, floating in the air and seeming to swim in the wind, to symbolise the masculine virtues. There is a temple where a great carp is said to have been fed, by the same family of hereditary carp-keepers, for nearly three centuries; I find it easier to believe that the family has been the same than that the carp has. And the devout Japanese Buddhists believe that fish can be eaten without sin, though mammals cannot, and therefore appreciate the carp on the table as much as any mediaeval monk in Lent, or on Friday. (Convergent cultural evolution has led the Japanese, again like the mediaeval Europeans, to insist on classifying whales and porpoises as fish, while relishing their meaty flavour; but they went one better, giving deer the honorary title of "mountain whale" and so letting themselves eat venison with a clear conscience.)

In Eastern Europe the carp is not worshipped but farmed in immense numbers, yielding a hundred thousand tons a year or more. There, too, its capture has long fascinated some; Dubravius of Moravia in his book on fish "telleth how, travelling by the highway side in Silesia, he found a Nobleman booted up to the groins, wading himself, pulling the nets, and labouring as much as any fisherman of them all: and when some belike objected to him the baseness of his office, he excused himself, that if other men might hunt Hares, why should not he hunt Carps? Many gentlemen in like sort with us will wade up to the armholes upon such occasions, and voluntarily undertake that, to satisfy their pleasure, which a poor man for a good stipend would scarce be hired to undergo" moralises Robert Burton in the *Anatomy of Melancholy*.

Britain by contrast is far from the carp's Asian home; the fish was not introduced here till quite late, possibly in the fourteenth century. The *Boke of St Albans* mentions carp as a rarity, "a dainty fish but I wot that there be but few in England". Nearly a century later, in *A book of fishing with Hooke and Line and all other instruments there unto belonging* (London, 1590) it is claimed that "The carp is also a straunge and dainty fish to take, his baits are not well known, for he hath not long beene in this realme. The first bringer of them into England (as I have been credibly enformed) was maister Mascoll of Plumsted in Sussex, who also brought first the planting of the Pippin in England." It is doubtful how far this should be believed; especially since the author of the work, identified on the title-page only by his initials, was none other than Mr Leonard Mascall, of Plumstead, who was elsewhere content to copy the *Boke of St Albans*, without acknowledgement.

Straunge and dainty, though, is a sound description of the fish and its pursuit. *Cyprinus carpio* is the quintessential cyprinid; drowsy, majestic, powerful, beautiful to its admirers; shy and cunning when pursued, valiant when caught. The origin of its name is unexplained; it appears in the sixth-century chronicler Cassiodorus as "a fish of the Danube region, *Carpus*"; the word, like the fish, coming from east of Europe. *Cyprinus* is the Greek form of the name; it may have taken that form after Venus the Cyprian goddess, to commemorate the carp's fertility; four to five hundred thousand eggs per pound in a female, who may have a third of her weight as ovaries; polyandrous, each female spawning with two or three males at a time. But as far as is known there is no real aphrodisiac effect of carp's meat, or any other fish's; eating fish on Friday, the day of Freya the Teutonic Venus, is just coincidence; and the monks who fed only on fish were not seeking to acquire additional virtue by overcoming additional temptation.

Since the carp, in Europe, has always been a semi-domesticated animal at least, it is found in the variety of different forms usually produced by artificial breeding. The wild carp are relatively slender, not much deeper-bodied in proportion to their length than a roach, and with the usual cyprinid armour of big overlapping scales, dark on the upper surface, metallic sides with a tinge of green or brown, pale on the belly, and with reddish or pink tints in the paired fins. The faster-growing artificial varieties have much deeper and more humped bodies; some of them, the mirror carp, have enormous distorted scales that may be scattered over the body or sometimes arranged in rows along the lateral line; at the base of the long dorsal fin the scales are normal. Between these big mirror scales the skin is bare, but tough. In the leather carp the scales have almost entirely vanished and the skin is everywhere like leather. There are also the golden or koi carp, a highly ornamental, oriental orange-gilt variety popular in parks. All these carps interbreed and produce offspring which may be intermediate between their parents, or may have the body shape of one and the skin of another. The distinctive features are always the large, smooth head with the four-barbelled, leathery mouth, and the big long dorsal with its sharp spiny first rays, rising to a crest at the front. When carp were introduced into Lake Ontario, they caused a panic; the great pointed dorsal fins of surface-cruising carp were mistaken for sharks.

Carp do not, I think, grow as big as sharks; their greatest real size is doubtful, but undoubtedly enormous. Mr Richard Walker's famous forty-four-pound Redmire carp cannot be the limit; there are, to put things cautiously, reports of carp over fifty pounds taken recently from waters whose locations are kept carefully secret from the profane multitude, and to which the venerated fish have been returned. And was not one seen in Redmire itself, as yet untaken, "looking like a bronzed rowing-boat", of inestimable weight? In June 1886 a great carp was taken from Lake Garda, near Lugano; thirty-two kilos (seventy pounds), the Italian anglers say. Paolo Giovio in the sixteenth century claimed that in nearby Lake Como they grew to two hundred pounds and were quite uncatchable, but could be shot with crossbows as they lay sunning themselves on the surface. And Charles Badham, a credulous naturalist of the last century, reported that a carp nine feet long and three feet deep was netted in the Oder near Frankfurt in 1711, but failed to notice that its supposed weight (seventy pounds, again) would only be possible if it was skeletally thin.

But the charm of carp fishing does not lie simply in the pursuit of giants. Carp are clever as well as big; to some extent, clever because they are big. A large fish has large eyes, with more cells in its retina, and can therefore make out fine details more clearly; a large cyprinid has a large swim-bladder, and therefore its Weberian ossicles move more in response to sound and its hearing is keener; and a large carp is an old, experienced adversary that is not easily deceived. Cyprinids have good memories; goldfish at least, presented with problems and mazes suitable for underwater animals, learn as well as laboratory rats, and there is no

Three tench in the mill-pond outside the studio

reason to suppose other cyprinids are less gifted. (Fish psychology is an infant science, and the fish are sometimes cleverer than the experimenters. A tropical fish was once found to respond to unbelievably weak sounds, swimming to the top of the tank to be fed whenever an electric bell was rung, no matter how faintly. Eventually a sceptic disconnected the bell from the button, and found that the fish still responded; then they realised that it had not been listening at all, but watching the movement of the experimenter's hands.)

Now the art of ground-baiting depends on exploiting the fish's memory; on teaching it that some unnatural substance which it can only get from you, bread or luncheon meat for instance, is an excellent food, and then deceiving it with a hooked morsel. With carp, any one bait on a particular water goes through three stages. First the fish don't know it's food; they have not been educated. Then they realise that it is food, and come to eat it. With care and persistence, they can be educated to come and take it from one particular spot; from your hand, if you persist long enough. Then lastly, in heavily fished waters where many hooked fish break away or are returned, the older ones become shy and doubtful, associating that bait with being caught. So when you hear that so-and-so has done wonders with some new bait, remember that he will not have mentioned the tedious days in which he threw the bait in but caught nothing with it; and that the same bait, later, may be quite neglected.

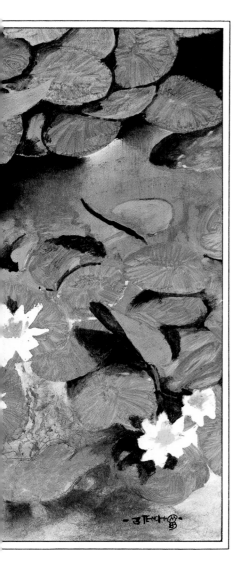

And as well as a carefully planned campaign of baiting, the carp fisher studies his prey's habits and movements with scientific dedication; and, since carp feed for choice in the hours of darkness, he keeps vigil through the night; a Tennysonian figure, alone with the trees and waters and the immense silences of the dark; haunting the margins of the misty lake, waiting for who knows what to reveal itself in the mysterious depths

> *where the great drowsy fins a moment rise*
> *Of fish that carry souls to Paradise*

which is Yeats, not Tennyson, and speaking of the dolphins of Byzantium not the carp of Redmire; and to judge by the haggard faces of some carp-fishers in the morning, Paradise is not where they have been. Even at night you must keep still and quiet, and feel the carp approaching; and to find it gone again, or lose it in the dark, is an addictive bitterness.

To lose a carp is all too easy; it cannot swim fast, not more than seven or eight body lengths per second, but it swims strongly and determinedly and can put its great weight into play. Worse, it nibbles and sucks at bait as tentatively as a bream does; sending up its own pattern of bubbles of very mixed sizes, some small and some as big as a golfball, when it burrows in the mud; picking bottom-lying bait up in its lips, and sometimes swimming away for a short distance with the bait held loosely, not attempting to eat it for a while, to the grief of the excited angler who strikes too soon. It is not certain why they do this; some say so as to take the bait out of the reach of other fish, much as a duck will run off with a piece of bread thrown to the flock; but carp, except when young or spawning, are rather solitary fish, that do not form tight competitive schools like bream. Also, its keen senses call for much lighter tackle than is comfortable with such a large fish; and for great discretion by the angler who will tackle the greatest challenge coarse fishing has to offer.

For centuries resolute souls have studied to improve the techniques of deceiving carp. Cassanius Bassus in the sixth century recommended a good all-purpose ground-bait which I dare say would have worked as well for carp as for any other fish; three limpet shells, with "Jehovah God of Armies" inscribed on them; but he does not say whether in Greek, Hebrew or Syriac. It's the details that count. Later, more realistic anglers tried a bewildering variety of bait, apart from the fairly obvious worms (still approved of) and maggots (rarely effective). Bread, or bread paste, is a bait that carp do not have to be taught about; but when carp were thought almost uncatchable save by nets, many sought to improve on such simplicity. "Of pastes for this fish," says Walton, almost despairingly, "there are as many as cures for toothache", but I doubt if they caused anything to be pulled out. Raw bullock's brains, which the angler should chew up till they can be easily moulded into pellets, was one unlikeable solution; or, better as emergency rations for the angler, green peas covered with melted butter; or, unsportingly, groundbait soaked in brandy so that the carp could be taken while befuddled; or more deviously, groundbait containing purgatives to make the carp ravenously hungry the next day. Richard Blome, whose mistitled *Gentleman's Recreation* (1686) gives the last hint, also devised the ultimate swimfeeder; an old door, covered with stiff clay a couple of inches thick, set with loosely-embedded beans which can be dosed with purgative or set with hooks.

Mr Henry Cholmondeley-Pennell, in his *Coarse Fishing* of 1885, claimed some success with a method which takes ground baiting to its logical conclusion. He left his rod propped up fully rigged, as usual, with a ball of paste or a worm on the hook, but with the point of the hook deliberately broken off, and replaced the bait as often as it was taken. After some days, when the carp were thoroughly educated, he also replaced the broken hook by a new, sharp one. Some would think that this method is obscurely unsatisfactory; like the modern device of using a radio-controlled battery-powered model motor-boat to tip your groundbait into the right spot, it isn't exactly cheating but. . .

Some modern devices have a long ancestry; the luminous Betalight float was anticipated by Robert Howlett, Esqre., Barrister-at-Law, whose *Angler's Sure Guide* of 1706 is full of ingenious inventions; he had obviously understood that carp must be taken when they most feed, in darkness, and had translucent swans-quill floats stuffed with glow-worms to help him register the bite. He also devised the forerunner of the bite alarm; he wound his line around a small forked stick, from which he suspended a hawk's bell, so as to give him notice if the fish bit when he was briefly distracted (as carp so often do). Howlett believed, too, in doubling his chances of taking a carp by having two hooks to his line, separated by a length of brass wire a foot long, with the line made fast to the middle of the wire. This would make for problems in casting; but Howlett was an eminently practical angler, the first to specify a series of runners on the underside of his rod (carefully placed brass loops, for him; who knows what they used before?) and there may have been something in it.

Modern carp, though, would surely shun such obvious tackle. The approved technique with a bottom bait nowadays is to have your rod pointing directly to the bait, the tip submerged even, so as to offer the fish no resistance as it picks up the bait; the movement of the line alerts the angler. Bread, big worms or potatoes, the last peculiarly excellent since they are largely proof against small fish, are recommended for bottom-feeding carp; floating crusts have captured many. But the full complexities of modern carp fishing, for cloopers and margin-patrollers and bubblers and smokescreeners and the elusive tenters, and the applied physics that make it possible to work out which part of the water will be at the carp's preferred feeding temperature, are unsurpassably described in Mr Richard Walker's *Still Water Angling*, which if you have not read you surely ought to.

Chinese grass-carp, the latest species successfully introduced to Britain

Overleaf
The Leviathan carp, strong, cunning, cautious; the great challenge to artist and angler

As great a wonder, in its way, as the skill of the carp-catcher is the carp's hardiness when caught; and that of the other cyprinids which can survive without breathing. It is natural that fish of warm, slow, stagnant, oxygen-depleted waters, that rarely exert themselves, should have little need for air; and in the ponds of south-east Asia, which appear to be the original home of the cyprinids, the summer waters must be depleted indeed. Carp and other still-water cyprinids can extract more oxygen from depleted waters than other fishes can; they have a special

form of haemoglobin, the red blood pigment that carries oxygen in the blood, which binds oxygen better than usual, so as the blood flows through their gills they absorb oxygen more thoroughly. But even when completely deprived of oxygen, cyprinids survive; the record is held by an Indian cyprinid, *Resbora daniconius*, one of which lasted one hundred and two days inside a hermetically sealed jar, with neither food nor air, and lost three-quarters of its weight before succumbing.

How do they do it? Well, all animals can manage without oxygen for a little; any sprinter does while he runs. Animals depend for energy mostly on glucose, which they burn (if they have oxygen) to form carbon dioxide and water. But if short of oxygen they can manage a more limited conversion of glucose to lactic acid; this provides much less energy, but needs no oxygen. A sprinter needs more energy than he can get oxygen for; so in his muscles he converts glucose to lactic acid, which, however, he can only stand in small doses. The pains in over-exerted muscles are due to lactic acid poisoning, and the panting of a runner after he has finished his race is due to his taking in more oxygen to burn up the lactic acid he has formed. There is a more efficient way of getting energy without oxygen; yeast cells when fermenting sugar in an air-tight container produce ethyl alcohol, which gives them lots of energy but which would derange their nervous system, if they had one. Carp, astonishingly, are self-fermenting fish; deprived of oxygen they produce a little lactic acid but mostly ethyl alcohol; and they pass most of it out into the water through their gills and stay largely sober. This is not the whole story; funny things happen to fats in their livers, which no-one fully understands; but alcohol production is the main response of carp and other still-water cyprinids to lack of air. (Men produce a little alcohol too, by fermentation in the bowels of even the most rigid teetotaller.)

I suppose that a captured carp, kept on wet sacking but unable to breathe much through the gills, and also unable to get rid of much alcohol through them, must be quite happy if it can take its mind off its strange surroundings.

Paradoxically, this ability to do without oxygen, which was developed so that fish could survive in hot, oxygen-poor water, has allowed some cyprinids to survive very cold winters as well. When ice forms, the water below is cut off from the air; and if snow lies on the ice, light cannot penetrate and the plants beneath the ice cannot produce oxygen by photosynthesis; in such circumstances, cold-loving fish like trout or pike will die. Carp do not die even in thickly-iced ponds, through a Polish or a Russian winter; they become inactive as the water gets colder, but they ferment gently and survive. Generally they cluster in holes in the deepest water, where the temperature stays at 4°C for as long as may be; they crowd together there, and are sometimes much afflicted by leeches and carp-lice, but on the other hand any worms in their guts starve to death as the carp go for months without feeding. They may lose fifteen per cent of their weight over the winter; specimen hunters should concentrate on autumn.

I am surprised that none of the early naturalists managed to confuse this huddled over-wintering of carp (and bream) with the supposed conglobulation of swallows and other migratory birds, that Robert Burton, for instance, thought "lie hid in the bottom of lakes and rivers, holding their breath, often so found by fishermen in Poland and Scandia, two together, mouth to mouth, wing to wing." Even so great a naturalist as Gilbert White was not convinced that swallows migrate; to imagine them converted into fish for the duration of winter would not have strained the mediaeval imagination. The Chinese, analogously, suppose that when the quail disappear in spring they are converted into moles; and the Japanese, that badgers can transform themselves into tea-kettles. (And according to Burton, again, "men . . . in Lucomoria, a province in Russia, lie fast asleep as dead all winter from the 27th of November, like frogs and swallows, benumbed with cold, but about the 24th of April in the spring they revive again, and go about their business.")

As long as cyprinids have a warm summer to breed in, though, they need not fear the winter's cold. Not usually, at any rate; though there have been some hard winters in which Italian carp, apparently a less hardy strain than the eastern European fish, have failed to survive in northern ponds. Some authors go further, and affirm that cyprinids can actually survive when the whole pond freezes; "it seems almost as incredible as the resurrection to an atheist," remarks Walton of one such story. A fish's blood will remain unfrozen when ice has formed around it, because of the materials dissolved in the blood; a carp's blood freezes at minus 0·6°C, perhaps less if it is laced with alcoholic antifreeze; so a fish might survive in ice, though hardly when its own blood crystallises. Yet some claims are very positive; Mr L.M. Turner, in 1886, described rigidly frozen Alaskan mudminnows, embedded in ice, being fed to huskies. "The pieces that are thrown to the ravenous dogs are eagerly swallowed; the animal heat of the dog's stomach thaws out the fish, whereupon its movements soon cause the dog to vomit it up alive. This I have *seen*," he emphasised. Experiments in the San Francisco aquarium have shown that these mudminnows (distant relatives of the pike, not cyprinids) do indeed move about after being thawed out from blocks of ice; but they die the next day.

So some of the stories of the marvellous resuscitation of carp may not be incredible. As for their equally marvellous longevity, often alleged, biologists are doubtful. Tame carp may live for fifty years or more; that they outlast the centuries is often proclaimed, never proved. Their habits are such as would encourage longevity; indolence, sleep and avoidance of oxygen, the necessary poison.

We are so accustomed to seeing coal and wood burn, and metals rust and tarnish, and fabrics fade, that we do not readily appreciate what an unusually vigorous, reactive chemical oxygen is; it slowly attacks the fabric of all living things; and the ingenious studies of Professor Harman, of Los Angeles, have led him to propose that the root cause of senile decay is irreversible damage, by oxygen, to the cells of the central nervous system. Animals, he thinks, age at different rates (a three-year-old mouse is old indeed) according to their abilities to withstand, and perhaps repair, the damage caused by air they breathe; and, perhaps, develop some diseases of old age (like cancer) because of the prolonged oxidation of their tissues. Certainly, anti-oxidant chemicals reduce the effects of carcinogens; and cells grown in special incubators with a reduced oxygen supply mutate less than in air. A carp, that lives its life in waters poor in oxygen, often manages without it altogether, and spends much of the year in cold storage beneath the ice, might be expected to survive better than an oxygen-demanding, active trout, soon to be burnt up. But the real record for underwater longevity, alas, is held not by the carp but by the lowly sea-anemone; some specimens, collected as adults some time before 1862, were presented to Edinburgh University, and remained in perfect health with no sign of age till 1940; when the assistant in charge of them, distracted by events of almost equal importance, forgot to change the water in their tank and brought them to a premature end.

I may never be forgiven for presenting recipes for the cooking of such a majestic fish as the carp; so I will only mention in passing that the Chinese have a most curious dish, carp cooked in mutton broth, an outstanding example of their skill at combining different flavours; and that the best European recipes come from the East, either directly or brought by immigrants, as in the French *carpe à la Juive*, in which the whole fish is served in a sweet-sour jelly with raisins and almonds. Chinese gourmets make a casserole from the head only, the oiliest part, and give the rest away.

There is also a ridiculous after-piece to follow such splendour, the Crucian carp, *Carassius carassius*, a worthy pigmy which no-one can take seriously. It is shaped like a carp, sometimes even more hump-backed, but without barbels; it is more closely related to the goldfish, *Carassius auratus* (and quite unrelated to *Carausius*, which is a stick-insect); it grows to a few pounds but is not much pursued in the various waters where it has been introduced, being quite overshadowed in reputation. It outdoes even the carp in hardiness in winter. This species had its moment of glory in Essen in Germany, in 1806, when a hailstone as large as a hen's egg was found to contain a small Crucian that had been swept up into the clouds by a waterspout, and frozen in the air. It is not recorded whether the fish revived on being thawed; I shouldn't wonder. But the Crucian will never have the allure of the true great carp. To draw up Leviathan with a hook is an old ambition.

Tiddlers

Serious adult anglers do not trouble themselves too much with the lesser fishes of the streams, leaving them to the care of small boys with nets and jamjars. There is no British rod-caught record for the stickleback, amazingly; and it is in many ways a mercy that sticklebacks do not grow very large. Like the shrews on land, they are tiny but ferocious; I saw one once kept in a tank with a two-pound roach which it bullied cruelly. The stickleback would get just above and well behind the roach, keeping in its blind spot, and dart forward to take a bite at its dorsal fin. After a few days they had to be separated.

That was a three-spined stickleback, *Gasterosteus aculeatus*, the best protected and so the most adventurous and aggressive of the family. They are a widespread group of fishes, found all across the northern parts of the globe, in fresh or salt water, all small but well armed. Many fish have a spiny, protective first dorsal fin; the sticklebacks have converted this to a row of separate spines, strong and sharp as thorns. The pelvic fins, too, are no longer used for steering but have become sharp spines, and the first ray of the anal fin is also spiny. This makes a stickleback a prickly mouthful for any predator; and in the three-spined variety the sides of the body are further protected by a row of overlapping bony plates. Professor Tinbergen at Oxford had a famous film of a young pike trying to cope with a small three-spined stickleback, snapping at it crossways but unable to pierce its armour, and unwilling to bite hard on the spines; eventually spitting it out in disgust, to swim away unharmed. Only hungry pike will even attempt to eat such a difficult morsel; placed in a tank with sticklebacks and small roach, pike eat all the roach first then starve for several days before starting on the spiny alternative.

So the stickleback is of little use as a bait for larger fish; pike and trout do occasionally take them, though, and any angler who finds himself with no other bait at all might benefit from the knowledge that trout go for either small or large specimens rather than middle-sized. (These terms are relative; "large" means three inches, "small" half that size.) The middling sticklebacks are the most manoeuverable, and are recognised by the trout as difficult targets and left alone. Fish have considerable knowledge of their prey; that is why it is useless to remove the spines of a stickleback to make it more attractive bait, as Daniel suggests; the trout expect the spines to be there and don't believe they are gone.

Thus protected, three-spined sticklebacks swim securely in all but very fast waters, feeding off any animal smaller than themselves. (A large stickleback was once seen to eat seventy-four young dace inside five hours.) In the south of Europe they are found in fresh water only; they stay inland in England; but along the northern Atlantic and Arctic

The male three-spined stickleback in his startling breeding colours

The stickleback: a prickly mouthful for any predator

coasts, in Shetland and the north of Scotland, they enter the sea in winter and return to the rivers in spring. Presumably the southern races were also migratory during the last ice age, but are now trapped for a while till the seas cool again. The more southerly, and the more inland races have fewer plates on their sides; far northern marine ones may have up to thirty, running right down to the tail fin, some freshwater ones may be quite bare.

The spring not only brings the northern marine sticklebacks up into fresh water; it sends them all from their usual drab brown into their flamboyant breeding livery; the male with bright blue eyes and vivid scarlet throat and belly, silver head and shimmering blue-green flanks, the female more discreetly pink beneath.

The nine- or ten-spined stickleback, *Pungitius pungitius*, is less conspicuous than the better-known three-spined species. It is a little smaller, with numerous weaker spines on the back and never any side armour; the breeding livery is more discreet, the male sporting only a black belly, white pelvic fins (or rather spines) and a red-tinged head. Being more vulnerable, it lurks in denser vegetation than the three-spined species usually frequents; and it builds its nest later in the year, in early summer when there is better cover. There is also a fourteen-spined species, occasionally drifting into brackish water but breeding in the sea.

The other prickly small fish of our streams is the miller's thumb, or bullhead, *Cottus gobio*; one of the North American family of sculpins that has spread to the old world. It is found throughout Europe north of the Mediterranean in cold, clear, fast-running water; but though very well provided with fins it swims as little as it can. Having no swim-bladder, it lies on the bottom, with the flattened toad-like head, from which it gets its name, offering little resistance to the current. By day it lurks under cover, in weeds or under stones, coming out to forage at night or on dull days. When it swims, it usually keeps its body still and rows itself along with strokes of its large, broad, spiny pectoral fins; the slender body and the tail and unpaired fins, also big and spiny, are used only for bursts of speed in emergencies. The fins, and the spikes on the gillcovers, are intended to deter predators; sometimes deterrence fails with catastrophic consequences for both parties. A grebe was once found dead on the banks of the Thames, with a bullhead stuck in its throat; kingfishers, too, have been impaled by their intended prey.

Bullheads themselves feed on insect larvae and fish eggs and fry, causing some annoyance in trout streams. There is a persistent legend that they themselves are well worth eating, despite their repulsive appearance and small size (four or five inches at most); some say that on boiling their flesh turns red like a salmon's, and is as delicious. "At least," said Mr Charles Badham, a Victorian naturalist, "those did that I took from the waters of the Lake of Neufchatel, when I was young." Angling romances, like flies, are best pitched fine and far off.

Asian in origin, rather than American, are the loaches; though the loach is not a Chinese roach, but more like a dwarf catfish. Two species have reached Britain; the stone loach, *Noemacheilus barbatulus*, and the spined loach, *Cobitis taenia*. The first is fairly widespread, the second

Kingfisher

restricted to East Anglia. The stone loach is sometimes as long as five or six inches; it has a rounded head and body, slightly extended nostrils and six long barbels round the mouth; the spined loach is smaller, with a sideways-flattened head and body, streamlined nostrils, very short barbels and two moveable, backward-pointing spines beneath each eye. Both are drably coloured, the spined loach with a row of dark spots down each side.

If you can get one a loach is not a bad live-bait, being very tenacious of life; but it is a nocturnal fish that burrows in the daytime and is hardly worth the trouble of taking. It is a pity that we do not have its European cousin, the pond loach or weatherfish, *Misgurnus fossilis*, an interesting fish that grows to eighteen inches and is very sensitive to changes in atmospheric pressure, rolling on the surface of ponds before thunderstorms. In stagnant water it also comes to the surface to swallow air, which it stores in a bulge of its intestine so as to absorb the oxygen into its blood. It expels the depleted air through its vent, with a characteristic popping noise.

There are two other small freshwater creatures which are fishes by courtesy, shellfish that is, that deserve a mention: the crayfish and the mussel. The "fish" in crayfish is there by mistake; the name in the old German tongue was *Krebiz*, a variant of *krebs* or crab; whence the English crayfish and French *écrevisse*. It is really a sort of small freshwater lobster; like the lobster, its shell has a mixture of pigments which give it a bluish-brown appearance when alive, but only the red pigment survives cooking. And like the lobster, it is delicious; but neglected in Britain, for it needs very clean water to flourish. It is very choosy in other ways too; it prefers streams that flow east-west, so as to give it shelter from the midday sun; and it likes lime-rich water.

In their chosen waters, crayfish scavenge by night as a rule. They lie up in deep burrows by day, and walk along the bottom in the dark, feeling and smelling their way. On their long antennae, and on their large claws, they have sensitive hair-cells sunk in little pits, which sense displacement in the water much as a fish's neuromasts do. They will eat whatever comes their way; pondweed roots, snails, eggs, larvae, dead fish. They cannot swim forwards, but if threatened they can clap their tails hard against their bellies, and leap backwards through the water.

In crayfish waters, a lowered net or trap in the evening or at night, baited with a little fresh meat or offal, will easily catch one or two; though not in winter, when they hibernate. Really dedicated anglers use their catch as bait for chub, which are very fond of crayfish tail; I call this heroic virtue, for crayfish are excellent food and chub are - well, we know what they are. Crayfish should be kept for a few days in clean water to purge them, if you have any doubts about the river from which they were taken; then pull out the bitter rear gut and simmer them in a stock made from cider or a mixture of wine and water, flavoured with carrot and onion (essential), shallot and celery (optional) with a bit of thyme, salt and a bay leaf. For real splendour, convert the cooked crayfish into Nantua sauce; a béchamel sauce with added butter and

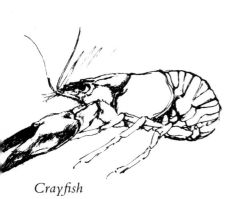

Crayfish

Miller's thumb, mussel shell, kingfisher's skull and pearl

blended crayfish meat, garnished with whole crayfish tails. The delicate combination of this sauce with pike or sole has to be tasted to be believed.

I don't know if you can cook freshwater mussels. They are nowhere as abundant as the anchored beds of sea-mussels, but probably they are edible, though the effort of gathering them is only worthwhile if they contain something far more worthwhile than flesh: pearls. One river species, *Margaritana margaritifera*, makes sizeable pearls; about one in three thousand has a valuable one, and the species is only found in a few regions. Nevertheless, British pearls were one of the lures that led the Romans here; without them we might have stayed a larger Ireland.

The pearl mussel grows up to six inches long and lives for over sixty years. The adult has a fairly uneventful life, lying on the bottom and sucking in water through a siphon, and filtering out the suspended plankton. One small European cyprinid, the bitterling, exploits this feeding system; a male bitterling in the breeding season will select a mussel (probably not a pearl one, but some other species), defend the territory around it and try to attract a female. One suitably seduced will insert the long tube which extends from her vent into the mussel's shell, and deposit a few eggs in its gills. The male then sheds his spawn into the mussel's siphon; it is drawn in and fertilises the eggs, which hatch a few weeks later, after developing in perfect security. The young stay inside the mussel's shell for a day or two, then swim away.

This remarkable way of spawning is really a cuckoo-like adaptation of the mussel's own breeding habits. Female mussels lay their own eggs in the gill cavity, and with their siphons suck in the spawn that nearby males release into the water. These eggs develop inside the shell to form tiny free-floating larvae, with a pair of gaping shells and a long thread-like tail, which drift out of the mother mussel when about a month old. Then comes the twist in the story of the interrelationship of mussels and fish; the larvae attach themselves to passing fish, perch or trout or barbel or what not, by their adhesive tails, and clasp on with their shells and burrow into the fins or gills (the scales elsewhere usually defeat them). The fish's tissues around these tiny parasites swell and form blisters, within whose fluids the larvae are nourished, grow and develop into small mussels shaped like the adults. The blisters burst, the small mussels fall out, the fishes swim on unharmed and the mussels crawl over the bottom till they find comfortable resting-places, often many miles from where they were born; far further than they could have travelled for themselves.

Since the truth can be so improbable, one can hardly blame the people of former ages for believing in the metamorphosis of horse-hairs into eels, or barnacles into geese.

Up from the Estuary

That a fish should swim from the sea up into fresh water, or from a river into the salt sea, is such a common occurrence that one hardly spares a thought for the strain that such a change imposes on the fish. We ourselves, when we swim in salt or fresh water, are not conscious of being dehydrated by the one or bloated by the other; but then we have a nearly impervious skin, and breathe air. But fishes, though their scaly skin is even thicker and more waterproof than ours, must draw a constant stream of water through their mouths and over the delicate membranes of their gills, to extract oxygen and unload carbon dioxide. Any membrane that will let such gases pass through readily must also be permeable to salts and water. The blood of a fish, like our own, is a dilute salt solution, not as strong as sea water. (This is worth remembering if you are ever cast away at sea; in principle at least, you can suck the juices of raw fish and survive without drinking. But stick to bony fish; the gristly sharks and skates boost their blood's strength with urea, so it more nearly balances sea water; this gives them a delicious kidney-like flavour, but ruins them as aids to survival.)

A bony fish in the sea always tends to take in salt through its mouth and gills, and to lose water (since the water is, in a sense, more concentrated inside the fish than outside). In fresh water, the same fish will leak salt and take in water. To counteract this flow, sea fish regularly swallow salt water, and then excrete the salt in a small amount of concentrated urine, and also through specialised excretory cells in the gills. In contrast, fish in fresh water can absorb salts through cells in their gills. Even "fresh" water has some salts dissolved in it, once it has seeped through the soil; only freshly-distilled rainwater is salt-free. Freshwater fish also pump out large amounts of water through kidneys, as a very dilute urine. When a fish moves from fresh to salt water, or *vice versa*, it has to alter the activities of its gills and kidneys. To some extent it can also partly compensate for the change in its surroundings by letting its blood salt concentration rise or fall a little. But the change from one system to another takes time; many species never attempt it, and would die if they tried. Migratory fish spend days or weeks in the estuaries, acclimatising themselves to the changed conditions; no wonder that such fish are reluctant to undertake any strenuous activity, which must increase the flow of water over their suffering gills.

Some migrants, like salmon, are so spectacularly prominent as they make their ascent that they are as familiar inland as any fish that spends all its life in the river; but several species slip up the rivers almost unnoticed, though worthy of the attention of the curious.

Few fish can match the flounder for his bizarre transformation and exemplary camouflage

The smelt, or sparling, *Osmerus epurlanus*, is one of these, a minor salmonid that ascends only just above the limits of brackish water to spawn; it breeds between February and April, rather late for a salmonid. It does not grow big, seven to eight inches at most. Its colouring is designed for marine camouflage, greenish-blue on the back and with pale silvery sides and belly, dull and lifeless compared to freshwater silver-sided fish; for the smelt's scales lack the reflecting crystals of guanine, and are almost transparent. When freshly caught, they have a purplish-blue iridescence, which soon fades.

What it lacks in colour it makes up for in scent, hence the name. Most people find it reminiscent of fresh cucumbers; Daniel says that those taken at Warrington in Cheshire have the best flavour, more closely resembling violets. The German varieties may be coarser, since the name in those parts is *Stinkfisch*, and the German naturalist Beneke describes it as having "a frightful odour of putrid cucumbers".

Smelt of one sort or another are found all along the northern coasts of Europe and Siberia. There are related species in the Pacific; one of these, *Thaleichthys pacificus*, the eulachon, takes the nutritious richness of the salmon family to extremes. Its flesh is so oily that a wind-dried eulachon is inflammable; the American Indians of the Pacific North-West used to set light to the tail and use it as a lamp; later they took from the white men the art of threading a wick through the body. Hence the eulachon's other name of candlefish.

In Britain the distribution of smelts is patchy; some come up the rivers of the eastern English coast, some are found in north Wales, others in the Shannon and irregularly in Ulster and in north-east and south-west Scotland. A split-dried smelt used to be a Scottish delicacy, taken as a relish with the morning dram of whisky; the people in Warrington should try it with their vodka, if any survive in the poisoned Mersey.

The smelt is hardly worth angling for; its greatest moment of glory was when one two-inch specimen provoked the great Trent zander panic. The other inconspicuous fish that comes up from the estuary to breed, the shad, will never be mistaken for anything but a herring. "Shad" in fact is an Anglo-Saxon borrowing (*sceadda*, it used to be) from the Celtic languages: the Welsh for herring is *ysgadan*, and the Gaelic *sgadan*. A shad is in fact a herring that breeds in fresh water; a member of a very old group of teleosts, well suited for feeding off plankton in the open sea. The rest of the herring family spawn at sea too, in great moonlit shoals twenty miles long, according to the envious testimony of fishermen who have seen all that wealth rolling on the surface. When the shad come up the rivers in springtime, they spawn after the herring fashion, between sunset and midnight, swimming vigorously close to the surface so that the shoal leaves an easily visible wake. And, like all herrings, they are mostly taken by drift-nets.

Shad are well worth angling for, though, if you can find them. There are two British species, the allice or allis shad (*Alosa alosa*) and the twaite shad (*A. fallax*). "Allis is a version of *alose*, the French name; so "allis shad" is literally "shad herring", or even if you like "herring herring".

(To an etymologist, there is something of the same absurdity in the names of the Avon and Axe and Exe and Don; innumerable anglers have fished in the waters of the River River.) "Twaite" is less intelligible; the French call it *l'alose finte*. I suspect that both these names, like the Linnaean species name, express annoyance that the twaite shad is the smaller but the more common of the two; and, say connoisseurs, the less tasty. The twaite is also distinguishable by the dark spots along its side, usually seven or eight, sometimes six or nine or ten, instead of the allis' one spot by the gillcover and few paler spots, one to four, behind. And the twaite, which feeds for choice on larval fishes among the plankton, straining them from the water it swallows, has on the front of each gill-arch about thirty gill-rakers, fine bony protrusions which hold the fry; the allis shad, which prefers the smaller marine crustaceans, has about eighty much finer ones. Even in fresh water, they both go for anything that resembles their marine food; anglers find small bright spinners or gaudy flies very effective bait. The real difficulty, nowadays, is finding the shad; the Severn and Wye were once famous for good allis, up to eight pounds weight some say, and the twaite were fairly widespread; now both are rarer than formerly.

This is a pity, for like all herrings the shad is fine food. The French serve it poached with *beurre blanc*, or baked with spinach or sorrel stuffing. On the other side of the herring pond, the American and Canadian shads (closely related species) are also highly esteemed; transatlantic recipes often call for the shad to be baked very gently for five or six hours to break up the bones, which as in all herrings can be a problem, especially if you cannot handle a knife and fork together. The Chinese of the lower Yangtse may be more dextrous with their chopsticks, for like the French (in this as in so many other respects) they await the yearly spring run of the shad with happy anticipation; and they steam it with vinegar or soy sauce or white wine. And the roe of all shad species is really excellent.

Sea basses enter estuaries, not rivers. They lack the colours of perches, having the standard silvery shades of free-swimming marine fish. (But colours can be added; the "record nine-pound perch" allegedly

Thick-lipped mullet, bass, shad, smelt and flounder

*Mullet browsing on the bottom
of moored boats*

taken from the Serpentine in the last century was rumoured to be a bass bought in Billingsgate, somewhat decorated.)

Bass can be cooked as if they were perch; or poached like salmon, or best of all filleted and fried in hot butter with lemon-juice. They can be angled for, also, as if they were perch, but unless they are well up the estuary you should not risk freshwater tackle. And the baits are very different: crab, squid, sand-eel, small flounder.

The last of these is itself well capable of entering an estuary and going further up the river than any bass. Flounders have been taken from the Rhine as far upstream as Basel, from the Severn at Shrewsbury, the Thames at Hampton Court, and even from the canalised Wavre near Waterloo (the battlefield, not the railway station). They enter fresh water only to feed; there, as at sea, they are excellently shaped for bottom feeding.

The shape of the flounder, and of the other related flatfish of the family Pleuronectidae, is one of the extravagant wonders of nature. All other vertebrates are pretty well symmetrical, externally at least. (The innards aren't; and they are less so in mammals, which have lopsided hearts and complicated layouts for the guts, than in fish.) In the flounder, and its more tasty cousins which avoid fresh water, all symmetry is lost; and the manner of its loss is as surprising as the final shape. All young flatfish hatch out of the egg as normal- looking, symmetrical larvae, vaguely related to the perches and so forth, deep-bodied with high pectoral fins and pelvic fins below or a little forward of them, and with long, soft-rayed dorsal and anal fins. They swim about in the usual way, in deep water well clear of the bottom, for weeks or months; then they sink to the bottom and alter astonishingly. The deep body becomes even thinner through, and deeper. And the bones, or rather the cartilage, of the skull twist; one eye and one nostril move down the cheek, the others come round over the top of the head to lie beside their fellows, the jaw shifts slightly: and the transfigured flatfish can now lie with what used to be one of its sides on the bottom, with both eyes looking up and with a very warped smile. The bones only harden after the shape has changed, which makes things easier. In flounders, the dorsal fin grows forward after the eyes have moved, till it nearly reaches the mouth; in some other flatfish, the dorsal fin extends first and the eye then moves up through it,

The spectacular bass leaping to free itself from the hooks of a spoon

which one would have thought was even more difficult. Flounders and soles generally lie on their left, others on their right; but there are a few specimens, and in some regions a local majority, of reversed orientation in many species.

This flat posture is very advantageous for a bottom-dwelling species; as can be seen from its independent evolution by a completely different group of fishes, the skates and rays, which have, however, flattened out sideways without contorting their features. A flattened fish can lie on the bottom well concealed, blending into the background; the flatfish improve this camouflage by a chameleon-like variability of colour. Their skin contains pigmented cells of different colours; by expanding and contracting different cells in different places, they can match the texture, uniform or finely or coarsely mottled, and the colour of the surface they lie on. Only the upper side changes colour, the lower is always pale. Flounders seem to match themselves to the bit of the surface they can see near their head. Placed with its head just over the edge of a dark area in a laboratory tank which has a white bottom elsewhere, a flounder goes dark all over; and one zoologist fitted his flounders with coloured spectacles and saw them rapidly adjust their colours accordingly. Their eyes, very sensibly, are sensitive to blue, green, yellow and red, alike.

The flattened shape may also help in swimming near the bottom. The side-to-side strokes of the tail and body that propel other fish are converted into up-and-down motions, sometimes with a rippling of the fringing fins; I do not know, but I suspect, that when a fish swims in this way near the bottom it gets the same sort of added thrust and lift that a very low-flying bird or aircraft gets from the "ground effect"; the fins, or wings, can interact with the solid immovable ground, even without their touching, and by having as it were something firm to push against can lift and propel the fish, bird or machine for less effort, or to more effect. (Flatfish need lift, since they have lost their swim-bladders, which are not needed when they lie on the bottom.)

But how this advantageous shape can have evolved is no small conundrum; if there were intermediate stages between the normal free-swimming symmetry and the warped bottom-living form, would they not have been remarkably unsuitable for both ways of life? Should we think rather of one dramatic mutation which produced a line of successful monsters? Or does one over-estimate the difficulties of a partly evolved flatfish? I thought they must be insuperable till I read of the Greenland halibut, which is less flattened than its cousins and which in shallow water swims as they do, but in deep water tilts over through ninety degrees to swim side-to-side, though with its head still skewed.

However their shape came about, the flatfish are one of the great gastronomic blessings of the sea; especially the soles, which alone among fishes improve in flavour with keeping, and the noble turbot. Unfortunately the flounder is among the less palatable of the flatfish; edible, but hardly worth cooking; easily caught, with a baited spoon or with any old scraps bounced along the bottom; trapped, even, in pits dug at low tide in which they lie after the ebb; but no great prize. Five pounds, and eighteen inches, is big for a flounder.

The only other common visitor from the sea, the grey mullet, is far more worth cooking, but damnably difficult to take with rod and line. The thick-lipped grey mullet, *Chelon labrosus*, is the most common British species; golden, thin-lipped and thick-lipped mullets are also to be found round our coasts, and there are about a hundred other species in the family, mostly tropical. They spawn in the sea, but enter rivers even as fry; they have been taken in unlikely places, as far upstream as Arundel. In appearance they are like a streamlined, graceful sea-bass; their spiny first dorsal and low pelvic fins well forward are reminiscent of perches, but actually their nearest relatives are the barracudas. Mullets, however, though fast swimmers as one would expect from their torpedo-like bodies and streamlined eyelids, are no predators. Their mouths are fringed with very small teeth which one would at first take for bristles; they feed on decaying animal or vegetable material which they suck out of the mud in shallow waters. They grind their food in their gizzards, rather than in their mouths.

This makes angling for mullet a most frustrating business. They will not refuse a bait, if it is fairly soggy; uncompressed bread does nicely; but rather than bite they will suck very gently at the bait till it disintegrates and leaves the hook bare.

Gastronomic authors are generally loud in praise of the mullet; but we must distinguish. The grey mullet is excellent eating, baked or fried, and its roe is (or ought to be) an essential ingredient of taramasalata; formerly, of the famous botargo, a relish which Pepys ate with bread and butter, and great draughts of claret. The red mullet, they say, is even better; but it is rarely found in northern waters, never of any size, and keeps to the sea. It is not very closely related to the other mullets (a different family; Mullidae, not Mugilidae); apart from the colour, it is easily distinguished by the two barbels on the chin with which it feels for food in the sea mud. It was the red mullet that was most highly esteemed by Roman epicures, both for its taste and for the iridescent shifting hues of its skin as it dies. Red mullets were placed in glass bowls on the table at Roman banquets, for the guests to admire the sight before the taste.

I do not know if it was a red or a grey mullet that the Romans traditionally thrust up the fundament of a convicted adulterer; Catullus says, with radishes. I suppose the punishment would have been worse with a weever.

Oddities

Not everybody knows that there swims in British rivers a fish with three eyes, one nostril and two-thirds of a pair of ears, that when young sees with its tail. Not everybody will believe this when they hear it; you could probably make a small but regular income betting on it, if you carried around with you a reliable work of reference or a well-dissected lamprey.

But this might only start off a series of arguments about what, exactly, counts as a fish, for the lamprey is very different from anything else an angler might hope to bring home; or rather, the lampreys are. There are three species in Britain; the sea lamprey, *Petromyzon marinus*, is the largest, two feet long at most when full grown; the river lamprey, *Lampetra fluviatilis*, is about half that size, and the brook lamprey, *Lampetra planeri*, does not grow over six inches. They all have the same body plan, the same primitive structures, but differ in their ways of life. They all breed in streams but move out downstream to various extents, like trout and salmon.

All lampreys are long, thin, wormlike creatures. The adults have a narrow fold of skin that forms a blunt fin at the end of their tail and two small, flattened, triangular dorsal fins, well back on the body; they swim with slow, clumsy, determined wriggles; they have no paired fins at all. Neither have they any jaws. Instead, their flattened sucker-like mouth has teeth, or rather sharp stout scales, all round it, and the powerful tongue carries a further battery of "teeth". The adult lamprey is specialised for holding on to a victim and boring away at its flesh, though not all adults do in fact feed. They make quite small wounds and suck mostly at the victim's juices; the lamprey's saliva contains anticoagulants to keep the blood flowing, as well as digestive juices to soften the meat.

The mouth is the largest part of the head; behind it are the two small dark visible eyes looking sidewards, with a single nostril on the top of the head, leading down invisibly in a deep blind channel to below the tiny brain. On either side of the brain are the internal ears, the balancing organs, also invisible from outside. When dissected they are found to have only two semi-circular canals, both vertical, one aligned forwards and one sideways; the horizontal canal present in all higher vertebrates is missing. I do not know how much this reduces their sense of balance; perhaps their lack of paired fins to use as horizontal stabilisers means that they could do little to restore lost balance, even if they could sense it. They have scattered exposed neuromasts arranged in unconnected lines.

Behind the nostril, covered with a thin layer of transparent skin but still with a retina and capable of perceiving light, is the third eye. Behind the eyes on each side is a row of seven prominent round dark holes; these

The lamprey is repulsive alive, delicious dead; the simplest of traps will catch many

155

look like yet further eyes, and were once believed to be so; but they are in fact the mouths of the breathing sacs. Lampreys do not have gills like other fishes; their way of feeding would make gills impossible, for a lamprey cannot take water in through its mouth while it is sucking and feeding, and it may remain attached to its victim for hours or days. Instead of gill-slits, it has these rounded sacs which open into its throat, through which it can pump water in and out while sucking with its mouth. This is not an efficient way of breathing, but a lamprey never takes much exercise.

When one adds that the lamprey's rudimentary skeleton is made of gristle, not bone, and its slimy skin is scaleless, one begins to regard the bet on the lamprey as a fish as being less than a certain winner; but in fact the lamprey is the degenerate descendant of a fish, and of a very bony fish indeed.

For the earliest of all fossil fish, the ostracoderms of over four hundred million years ago, shared many of the lamprey's characteristic structures but had their heads and fore-bodies encased in bone. These were not parasites but bottom-feeders, that used their jawless mouths to filter small items of food from the mud; they swam with finned tails, but had no paired fins; their gills were a series of holes rather than slits; they too had a single nostril and had a small eye on either side of their head and a third above, peeping between two plates of bone to cover the blind spot above. And some of their fossils have been so well preserved that they can be dissected, not with scalpels but by grinding away one thin layer of stone after another; and the inner ear of ostracoderms proves to have only two semi-circular canals, as in lampreys.

Ostracoderms were replaced long ago by fish with jaws and fins and gill-slits, the ancestors of all modern vertebrates which have acquired another dimension of balance and found two eyes adequate. The third eye survives as the pineal body, a small gland buried deep in between the lobes of the brain, that has no retinal structures remaining but when examined under the microscope is seen to have cells that are recognisably like cones. It is still capable of detecting the fraction of sunlight which penetrates the skin and skull and brain, and controls the way animals respond to the long summer days and winter nights, and in light-avoiding fishes seems to be the organ with which they sense the general brightness or darkness of their surroundings.

Lampreys, then, are a most ancient fish that have become specialised for parasitism at an unknown but very early date. Only one species of fossil lamprey is known, two hundred and eighty million years old from the Permian rocks of Illinois; between then and now, a long silence. If lampreys were found only in some remote wilderness, their discovery would have been a scientific sensation; as it is, familiarity breeds contempt.

Their feeding habits do not exactly breed affection, either, though they are less repulsive than their marine relatives, the hagfishes, which bore through into their victims' guts and leave them a bag of skin and bone. Hagfishes are even slimier, too; one caught and put into a bucket of water will convert all the bucket to a mess of slime. (They tie overhand knots in themselves, and pull themselves through the knot, to scrape off unwanted slime; and some tie only right-handed, others left-handed knots. Handedness came before any limbs.) Nor do lampreys, like vampire bats, add insult to injury by urinating over their victims before they depart; though indeed the bat has to shed most of the weight of the blood it sucks if it is to be capable of flight.

And in the early stages of their lives lampreys are quite innocuous. Their eggs hatch out into larvae as different from the adults as a tadpole from a frog; these are called prides colloquially, and at one time classified as different species from the adult (*Ammocoetes branchialis*) till their metamorphosis was observed. Prides are eyeless, finless, tongueless, pale grey or brown wormlike things with toothless horseshoe-shaped mouths, a quarter of an inch long when newly hatched. They drift downstream from the nests in the small streams where they hatch, and make J-shaped burrows in sandy silt or mud, where they live for some years, filtering minute organisms from the water and slowly growing to a length of three to five inches. Though eyeless, they have light-sensitive cells in their tails, and burrow tail-first into the mud if dislodged. (The skin of their tail contains porphyropsin, and the signal seems to be carried by the same nerves as serve the neuromast cells; the senses of primitive beasts are most irregular.) Their pineal eye can also detect light, and controls their regular colour change, pale by night and dark by day. When fully grown, they transform into adult lampreys, blue-grey above and silver-white beneath, sometimes with a rather attractive metallic violet glint on the sides, and leave their burrows; brook lampreys in early summer, from May to June, the other species later.

Adult river lampreys move further downstream and feed for two or three years, sea lampreys drift right out to sea or into big lakes, perhaps for longer. Tagged sea lampreys have been caught a hundred and fifty miles from their home river, and as deep as three thousand feet. A mature adult is marbled on its upper surfaces with a black or dark brown pattern. In spring mature sea lampreys gather in the estuaries and change into their breeding livery of bronze or orange or golden brown patches, the males with a thick rope-like ridge along their back; they make their way upstream for two hundred miles or more, travelling at night, to the spawning streams. The main runs in Britain are in May and June; they are followed in autumn by the river lampreys, and by brook lampreys which do not have an adult feeding stage but migrate soon after they leave their burrows. A migrating lamprey can make its way up a waterfall that would baffle a salmon; it will get underneath the flow and creep its way up a six-foot vertical drop, holding on with its mouth.

When the lampreys arrive in the breeding grounds in gravelly streams they build nests. They thrash out sand with their bodies and carry stones with their mouth-suckers to build oval pits, with U-shaped walls pointing upstream; hence *Petromyzon*, the stone-sucker, and *Lampetra*, whence lamprey, the stone-licker. A pair of big sea lampreys will move twenty-five pounds of material to create a nest three feet across. They mate in the nest, sea lampreys often monogamously, the others in huddles of a dozen or more, the male wrapping himself around the female, spawning at intervals of about five minutes for up to three days before they die exhausted and drift downstream. The eggs hatch among the stones of the nest, and the embryos remain in its protection for two or three weeks, just as trout or salmon fry shelter in their gravel redds.

I confess I have never eaten lamprey; but they have had a high reputation. A million a year were taken from the Thames at the end of the last century, forty-five million from the Volga. But extreme partiality for lampreys does seem to be a sign of a dubious character; King John, almost unparalleled for his misgovernance of England, once fined the city of Gloucester forty marks for failing to provide a lamprey pie for his feasts; but, legend to the contrary, the chronicles do not say he died of a surfeit of lamprey. And Pope Leo X, an ardent huntsman and practical joker, "a scoffing pope and an atheist", according to Robert Burton, had an exquisite rich sauce for lampreys which he would occasionally serve to his cardinals, spread over lengths of old rope.

Several fish also agree that the lamprey is delicious. I have mentioned their effect on chub; American fishermen say that brook lampreys are a bait for trout even more irresistible than salmon roe. They can be captured at any weir during the upstream migration, in narrow-mouthed tightly-woven baskets of willow or some more modern equivalent, set pointing downstream; they are not intelligent enough to work their way out.

Atlantic sturgeon

The other very ancient fish of British rivers, now extremely rare, is

the sturgeon, the only member we have of the classes of bony fish that date back to the Devonian. In that distant era three distantly related types started to gulp air; lungfish, lobefins, and ray-finned palaeoniscoids. A few of the others have likewise survived, so odd as to be worth a mention. Lungfish remain as eel-like forms in the seasonal tropical rivers of Australia, Africa and South America (the separated relics of the great southern continent). The African lungfish is memorable for its ability to survive droughts; it burrows into the mud before it dries, and remains inside its hardened nest without water for years if need be, somnolent, breathing air and building up amazing concentrations of waste materials in its blood, two per cent of urea or more; yet in the New York aquarium one was killed by the tapwater.

Lobefins' descendants survive as land vertebrates, but the fishes were thought to have died out towards the end of the age of reptiles, seventy million years ago. Their sole survivor, the Coelacanth *Latimeria*, caused great excitement when it was trawled up from the depths of the Mozambique Channel. The native fishermen of the Comoro Islands value its scales for repairing bicycle punctures.

Palaeoniscoids, like lobefins, gave rise to descendants which became abundant: the holostean fishes (now restricted to the great ancient rivers of the Mississippi and the Yangtse) which in turn gave rise to the modern ubiquitous teleosts. The sturgeons are one order of palaeoniscoid which have survived, like the lampreys, by specialising in one mode of feeding; they are big bottom-feeding fishes which feel into mud and silt with their long barbels, suck it up through their tube-like underslung mouth, pulp it and spit out the inedible bits. Hence the name, from the Anglo-Saxon *styrian*, the stirrer.

There are about two dozen species of sturgeon, found all over the colder parts of the northern hemisphere; only one, *Acipenser sturio*, the Atlantic sturgeon, has been found in Britain. Recognisable Acipenserid fossils go back sixty million years or more, to the Cretaceous when the last dinosaurs flourished and modern trees like oaks had appeared. They have lost most of their bone; the skeleton is of gristle, but five rows of great bony plates, a mark of the palaeoniscoids, run down their body. The tail, too, is of ancient design, with the backbone bent up so as to run along the swept-back upper lobe, and with a shorter, deeper lower lobe. All fish had such tails, which provide lift as well as thrust as the fish swims, before swim-bladders were developed to give lift; sturgeons have bladders, but keep the old tail; teleosts have equally-proportioned tail fins which give more efficient thrust.

Adult sturgeons feed in the sea or in large lakes, but come up rivers in spring or autumn, and spawn in early summer, below waterfalls for choice. Young sturgeons spend some time in rivers; Atlantic sturgeons remain for up to four years, feeding off worms and insect larvae, growing to around sixteen inches before they descend to open waters. After seven to fourteen years more they are mature and ascend rivers for their first spawning run, returning every year for decades if they survive, growing larger each year. The biggest Atlantic sturgeon recorded was eleven feet four inches and weighed seven hundred pounds; a tiddler of three hundred and thirty-eight pounds provided the biggest British rod-caught freshwater fish in 1933, to an angler in search of salmon in the river Towy in Wales, a Mr Alexander Allen. At first he thought he had hooked a log, but then the log got up and swam upstream. Aided by the intrinsic inefficiency of the palaeoniscid tail (which is nevertheless a formidable weapon: a blow from it can cut a man's arm to the bone), after some struggle he battered it into submission with a boulder. There followed further struggles with the Civil Service, which like the sturgeon has antediluvian affinities; for all sturgeons, whales or porpoises caught off Britain are Fishes Royal, property of the Crown. Eventually Mr Allen managed to sell his catch for fifty shillings, a small reward for such a feat.

Mediaeval royalty knew what they were doing when they annexed sturgeon. Their meat can be dressed to resemble pork, lamb or chicken; and the unripe eggs produce the delicate caviare, not appreciated in England till the Elizabethan merchants became acquainted with Russia. The best caviare comes from the fabulous beluga of the Volga and Caspian, which grow so big they suck up carp and salmon. A twenty-eight-foot beluga weighing two thousand eight hundred and sixty pounds was netted in the Volga in 1922, which produced three hundred and twenty pounds of eggs; and there are fairly credible records from the last century of one-and-a-half ton specimens. Beluga do not mature till eighteen or twenty years old; who knows how long they took to grow to such a size? Modern fishery biologists reckon to determine a sturgeon's age from the number of annual rings formed in its gill covers; a two hundred and eight pound lake sturgeon, netted in the Lake of the Woods in Canada in 1953, had one hundred and fifty two rings, which would put its birth before Trafalgar. Lake sturgeon grow more slowly than beluga; even so, the biggest taken of that species was three hundred and ten pounds. Nobody counted its rings.

Recently it has proved possible to strip the eggs from living sturgeon and return them to the water, as for trout, so caviare can be made without killing the fish. (I doubt if this has been tried on the big beluga, though.) The roe is rubbed through a screen to remove the membranes, mixed with salt, and packed after the brine has been drained off. There was some commotion in Russia in 1981 when tins appearing to contain smoked herring, intended for export to the West, were supplied to Soviet shops by mistake and found to contain caviare. One customer, ungrateful for such bounty, started enquiries which led to the arrest of a couple of hundred of the employees of the Ministry of Fisheries and to the end of the enterprising career of Comrade Vladimir Rykov, deputy Minister, who departed this life in front of a firing squad after being unable to persuade the investigators that anyone more senior was involved. A sad progression: Rykov, rakeoff, write-off.

The other product of the sturgeon, at times more valuable than caviare, is isinglass, the clear pure gelatin extracted from the swim-bladder. (The name, like buoy and yacht and skipper, comes from the amphibious Dutch; *huysen blasse* means sturgeon bladder.) In the days

The wels in water crowfoot: the least lovely of fishes

before synthetic compounds it was invaluable for clarifying beer, preserving eggs, cementing pottery and waterproofing fabrics.

It is fortunate that we can now make replacements, for the sturgeons are near extinction in many places. Weirs and dams block their migration, breeding grounds become polluted; and like all large, slow-maturing wild animals they are vulnerable to inadvertent over-cropping. When the unbelievable natural wealth of North America was plundered in the last century, sturgeon taken in the rivers of Ontario were piled like timber on the quaysides, to dry till they could be burned as fuel for steamboats. Now few remain, and of diminished size; and in western Europe outside Spain and Scandinavia they are almost gone.

The burbot, too, has all but vanished from Britain; has been vanishing for some time, for it is a northern fish that needs very cold, clear but not fast-flowing water to spawn in. Burbot breed in midwinter, in water not warmer than 35°F; ten or more of them group together to form a writhing ball, intertwined and constantly moving, which rolls along the gravelly bottom. And the burbot cannot survive summer temperatures of over 74°F; it is an ice-age relic that could not hide in the lakes. Cities and drainage improvements have driven it out; it used to lurk in the east-flowing rivers south of Durham and north of Suffolk that once drained into the Rhine.

It is the only freshwater member of the cod family, looking very like a ling; big gaping mouth with fine close-set teeth, barbel on the chin, pelvic fins in front of the pectorals, long tapering body with large ribbon-like dorsal and anal fins and a small rounded tail. "They are called the Nonesuch," said William Plot in his *Natural History of Staffordshire*, in 1686, "from the oddness of shape and the rarity of meeting them." Other names are eel-pout, and in Canada lake-lawyer, from their slippery evasiveness if one tries to grasp them or pin them down; the Linnaean name is *Lota lota*. An eight pound specimen was once caught in the Trent; in Siberia (where their skins have been used instead of glass in windows) they reach five feet, and seventy-five pounds.

Burbot are voracious predators; a fifteen-inch one was once found trying to swallow a twelve-inch walleye pike. Their flesh is white, firm and delicate, somewhat muddy in summer; the liver is as oily and nutritious as a cod's. In Queen Elizabeth I's time they were so plentiful in the undrained Fens that they were fed to the hogs; a few may yet survive in the bleak wastes of East Anglia. (There was a Fenland Ecology Party in Cambridge that aimed to restore the area to its former state of inundation; their motto, "Pull your finger out"; but I fear that like the Oxford Invade And Conquer France Society, which never achieved more than a day trip to Boulogne, they were largely a drinking club.) Burbot feed at night, and are most active in cold weather, lying concealed and somnolent in summer; so they are only likely to be taken at times when all sensible people are indoors. But a hardy angler who finds something mysterious, elongated but not an eel, removing his bait in the freezing fenland night, can console himself with the thought that he may have glimpsed the last of the English burbot.

In summer nights, if an angler in those parts catches a long, barbelled mysterious fish it is more likely to be the European catfish, or wels, *Silurus glanis*, another ugly, destructive, unwelcome and unremovable immigrant for which, like the zander, we have the Dukes of Bedford to thank. First introduced in Woburn, it is gradually spreading, or being spread, across the muddy waters of lowland England, where it thrives; the rod-caught record is forty-three and a half pounds. But there is still much room for improvement; there is an authentic record of one taken from the river Dnieper, of three hundred and six kilos (six hundred and seventy-five pounds), over fifteen feet long.

Catfish are also among the ugliest of fishes, and the most sinister. Pike are merely predatory; a wels rising from dark waters has a look of alien, powerful, profound malevolence. The great thick-lipped mouth gapes across the dark leathery face, the small wideset eyes glitter in the flattened head; an Idi Amin among fishes. The unnatural long barbels quiver forwards or sweep back as it rushes on; the mottled body stretches back and back, glistening bare and scaleless above but extraordinarily fringed with a long anal fin below, almost merging with the blunt tail. Not a fast swimmer, nor a fish of rapid waters, but capable of great strength. "It ran out my line for a hundred feet," is a frequent complaint in lakes where it has been introduced, "and then it smashed me, so I think it must have been a wels.'' They are omnivorous predators; bream, tench, roach, frogs, water-voles, ducklings, all are devoured. Those anglers setting out in deliberate search of this fish have need of stout tackle; but almost any juicy bait will do, worm or fish or frog, cast near cover in muddy water and preferably in the dark. It feeds, as it breeds, in summer and lies up in the cold weather. The main problem is that wels waters are usually eel waters, and though the wels keep the eels down they are usually outnumbered, so bait for one attracts the other. In the Danube they catch wels with a piece of oilcloth flapping on a hook; I do not know why this works.

Perhaps the wels' very acute hearing attracts it to the flapping cloth. Like the cyprinids which are the most closely related order, catfish hear very well through their swim-bladder and Weberian ossicles; perhaps even better than cyprinids, since they have a gap in the muscles of their body wall which lets part of the swim-bladder lie directly under the skin where it will be most sensitive to soundwaves in the water. Like cyprinids, too, the wels has a leathery mouth and pharyngeal teeth. It is said to be a popular dish in Europe, but I cannot say how it is served. There are various popular European stories, too, of the wels' feats: of the Hungarian angler who ran for three miles upstream by the treeless banks of the Danube, with a giant wels in play; of German wildfowlers who, instead of claiming to have seen waterfowl snatched under by giant pike, report the loss of their retrievers; Slavonic claims of child-eaters, man-eaters, horse-eaters . . . I repeat, they grow to fifteen feet. Aelian, who first recorded the art of fly-fishing, has a passage on the great Silurus of the Danube, that is taken on a line held by a team of oxen; when I first read it I thought it deserved to be true, and when I consider the reelless rods of Aelian's day I suspect it may be.

The only close relative of the wels is Aristotle's catfish, *Silurus aristotelis*, found in the basin of the Akhelos river in southern Greece; a dwarf form, never much over three hundred pounds, with only two barbels below and two above its mouth, unlike the wels' four below. I do not know if it was of this species or of the wels that Aristotle wrote that it is a fish unusually vulnerable to storms, often to be found floating thunderstruck on the surface. American bullhead catfish, species of *Ictalurus*, some of which have been released on the Continent, are small and only distantly related, quite fishlike, with none of the wels' nightmare power.

I have heard of the angling book that contains the correction, ''For cat-eating frogfish read frog-eating catfish'', but I have not been able to trace it.

EEL
(Anguilla Anguilla)

The Mysterious Eel

The European eel, *Anguila anguilla*, is the strangest of fish. Its blood is a deadly poison; it can crawl over land for surprising distances although it has no lungs; and, as generations of fish-gutters have known, it has no perceptible sexual organs, yet it breeds prolifically. How it does so has been much disputed for over two thousand years.

The middle stages of an eel's life are straightforward. Early every year small eels, or elvers, appear in estuaries and swarm upstream; sometimes in enormous numbers on the Atlantic coasts, less so in the western Mediterranean, and rarely in the eastern. Once in the rivers and lakes, they feed and grow for several years as "yellow eels", dull green above and dull yellow below, with fatty and very nourishing flesh. Every autumn some mature yellow eels change colour; their backs darken to black, their flanks become bronze and their bellies silver, and these "silver eels" flock down the rivers to the seas. The obvious conclusions to draw from this are that the eels breed somewhere in the sea, and that they can profitably be caught wholesale in their seasonal migrations. The first conclusion was, oddly, delayed; the second was reached in many countries before recorded history, and is still generally accepted.

About seventeen thousand tons of eels are caught each year in Europe; the most effective method is the fixed net or trap into which the eels swim. But the list of other methods is as endless as the ingenuity of fishermen. Elvers have been taken, in the dense masses in which they ascend favoured rivers, in nets or sieves or canvas scoops, or by brushing them off weirs into sacks spread at their bases. Only yellow eels can be taken with baits; the others are too keen on their migration to feed. Some stout characters spear them; this method can be messy in unskilled hands. Sir Jonah Barrington, the distinguished ancestor of the squash player, tells of an Irishman who grasped the spear far too near the blade, threw back his arm, lunged violently at an eel on his left side and removed his own head.

Fishermen may have realised that the migrating eels they caught were going to and from their breeding grounds, if they bothered to think of such things. Some scientists, impressed by the apparent absence of sex organs, decided that eels did not breed at all. This error, like so much else, can be traced back to Aristotle, who noted, correctly, that the sex organs are difficult to distinguish, and who may have believed that eels are formed by "spontaneous generation"; an interesting theory now defunct. Before microscopes were invented, the origin of many animals was mysterious, and generally attributed to spontaneous generation.

Many an angler thinking to play a four-pound bream has landed a half-pound eel: surely the least loved of fish

Maggots, for instance, appear in rotten meat in a way that – to those unable to detect the small eggs laid by flies – look like a spontaneous conversion of dead meat into living maggot. Aristotle may have thought that eels were similarly generated from rotting mud. At least, he said that they appear from the mud of pools after rain (quite true; eels survive drought buried in mud); and also that they come by putrefaction from the bowels of the earth. For generations this sentence was taken as committing the authority of the Father of Zoology in support of the theory of spontaneous generation.

Now that the theory has perished, classicists who wish to preserve the reputation of the classics point out that the Greek phrase usually translated as "the bowels of the earth" could mean "worms in the mud", and that elvers do indeed look like worms, hide themselves in mud, and give rise to eels. We can forgive Aristotle his mistake, if such it was; Greece is a bad country to study eels in, and he had very many other things to worry about, Alexander the Great not least. Other classical authors said little of value about eels, which they confused fairly thoroughly with congers and morays (which are related marine species) and lampreys (which are not). Exactly which species the Roman senators fattened for the table on living slaves is uncertain – as is the story. Pliny, who could believe anything, thought that eels reproduced by rubbing themselves to bits on rocks, with a new eel formed from each fragment. He also established an angling record, of sorts, with his account of the three-hundred-foot eels of the Ganges. Came the barbarians and the dark ages; fishermen went on catching eels, ignorant of Aristotle, but with vast efficiency. One village of twenty men, near well-named Ely, is mentioned in the chronicles as supplying sixty thousand eels a year to the Abbey.

In the twelfth century the mass of Greek learning returned to western Europe. Aristotle was at first in ill favour. The University of Paris in 1215 forbade him to be studied, for he was thought to support the ideas of one Amaury of Bène, a noted theologian recently accused of heresy. Amaury had died some time earlier; generally a bad tactical move even in university politics. They dug him up and burned his books with him. Despite this introduction to academic life, Aristotle was soon back on the syllabus – more exactly, for many subjects he was the syllabus. It is perhaps surprising that his discussion of eels survived translation from Greek into Syrian and Arabic, languages of eel-less countries; and then into Latin: but the dogma of spontaneous generation of eels came across. The belief that they were spontaneously generated from horse-hairs in streams seems to be western European addition. The simultaneous, perhaps contradictory, belief that eels engage in unnatural intercourse with snakes, still believed in France, dates back to classical times: Oppian in the second century added the details that the snake first empties his poison glands out of courtesy, and that if detected in his vicious practices he kills himself. Walton was intelligently dubious about the whole matter, adding the suggestion that elvers might condense from dew-drops, but recording that some held that eels must breed though they have no organs of generation that we can see.

After Aristotle had been proved wrong about many other matters, his authority on the breeding habits of eels was challenged. The eminent Dutch microscopist, van Leeuwenhoek, proclaimed in 1652 that he had found the eel's womb, and that it gave birth to living young; contrary to the unfashionable, scholastic dogma of Aristotle. In fact, he had dissected the bladder of an eel badly infested with threadworms; but since he was an illustrious modern authority his discovery stayed in circulation until the nineteenth century.

But real progress was made meanwhile; and all the discoveries about eels, till this century, were made in Italy. That country produced Redi, who first put in print the idea that eels must breed in the sea, and that the supposed young eels were worms; Mondini who suggested after microscopic investigations that the pale frilly ribbons that run through the abdomen are not fat deposits, as usually supposed, but the much sought after ovaries, only partly developed; and the great Spallanzani who studied the eel fisheries of the lagoons of Comacchio, where one hundred and fifty-two million gutted eels failed to reveal any visible eggs or young. And Szyrski, a Pole working in Trieste, first observed the undeveloped testes, nearly a century after Mondini. Sexist prejudice had led earlier zoologists to look for testes in the larger eels, which are all females. Then towards the end of the eighteenth century the Italians realised the rewards to be found in the Straits of Messina, between Sicily and the mainland, where violent currents throw up fishes from great depths. A strange, transparent, leaf-shaped fish, given the name *Leptocephalus brevirostris*, had earlier been found washed up on the beaches of Messina; Grassi and Calandruccio suggested in 1893 that the leptocephalus had the structure one might expect in a larval eel (except that the anus is in the wrong place, far too far aft.) And in 1896 they astonished the scientific world by capturing in the Straits a half-metamorphosed, intermediate form (in which the anus was migrating forwards.) And they even observed a leptocephalus changing into an elver in their aquarium. The next year the Straits yielded them a sexually mature male with unmistakeable testes. The mystery seemed solved; eels develop their sexual organs, and breed, in the depths of the sea, though exactly where was uncertain. The Italians supposed that their eels bred off Italy.

But soon after, a Danish zoologist, Johannes Schmidt, prepared a fierce blow to Italian national pride. He caught leptocephali from the deep waters of the Atlantic, and found that these were on average smaller than Mediterranean ones near Italy; and the further south-west he went, the smaller and younger they became. Eventually, in 1922, after eighteen years' search, he found the spawning ground where the smallest leptocephali occur; over very deep water in the Sargasso Sea, near the famous Bermuda Triangle about which so much profitable fiction has been written for the distraction of the feeble-minded. (It is pure coincidence that Schmidt's first voyage to the area ended in shipwreck.) From this place the Gulf Stream carries the leptocephali eastwards, over a period of two and a half years, to the European continental shelf and metamorphosis. It is odd that it takes them so long;

one-year-old turtles have been carried by the same currents from Mexico to the Severn; perhaps the leptocephali swim against the flow.

It still remained a mystery, though, how the adults travelled from Europe to the Sargasso. At great depths, obviously; for while yellow eels are practically blind, silver eels develop large, functioning eyes with blue-sensitive visual pigments of the kind found in deep-sea fishes. (Travellers allege that eels living in total darkness also develop bulging eyes, as in the *chiavicarole* of the old Roman sewers, an Italian delicacy.)

As the eel is a very efficient slow-speed, long-distance swimmer – its slime reduces turbulence in the water around it, its undulating motion pushes a large, slow stream of water behind it, which requires less energy than the small high-velocity stream produced by a normal tailed fish – it was supposed that the European eels could swim, perhaps using favourable deep currents, to the spawning ground in a few months; to spawn in spring, when the leptocephali appear, and then die. How they found their way remained a mystery.

The breeding habits of the eels of other parts of the world were not studied till after Schmidt's discoveries. It turns out that all eels need to breed over very deep, fairly warm water; why, no-one knows. In the great northern and southern ocean basins there are permanent rotating currents, like the Gulf Stream, which allow leptocephali spawned at suitable sites to be carried to distant lands. The Australian eel and the New Zealand eel have their spawning ground in the south-west Pacific; the Japanese eel, which also reaches the China coast, in the north-west Pacific; the American eel in the south-west Atlantic, a little south of the European eel. The south Atlantic waters are too cold for eels to spawn; the Pacific coast of America is perhaps too far from the spawning grounds.

In the tropics there are no great rotating currents. Tropical eels are found only where there is deep water near the coast, for the leptocephali have to swim rather than take a lift; and unlike the freshwater eels of temperate lands, tropical eels exist in many species. The greatest variety are found in the Indian ocean, thought to be the ancestral home of all eels. The marine conger eels are thought to breed over deep waters, with spawning grounds between Gibraltar and the Azores, and in the Mediterranean; but moray eels spawn in shallow coastal waters, within a hundred fathoms. *Enchelycore nigricans*, a marine eel of the tropical Atlantic, migrates in the reverse direction to the European eel; the adults live in the Gulf of Mexico, off the South American coast, and along the African coast to the Cameroons, but have their spawning grounds off the Cape Verde Islands.

All eels, freshwater or marine, have the characteristic leaf-like leptocephalus larva; a form they share, oddly, with the big-scaled, fast-swimming tarpon, the most spectacular leaper of the game fish, and presumably their least distant relative. Some distance; fossil eels have been found from seventy million years ago. These were primitive forms which still kept the pelvic fins their descendants have lost. Morays have found pectorals superfluous also.

One of the minor mysteries of the eel is the case of the giant leptocephalus; a specimen nearly six feet long was caught by Schmidt's *Dana*, in the South Atlantic in 1930. A full-sized leptocephalus that will grow into a six-foot eel measures less than three inches; should the giant mature in similar proportions, it could grow to two hundred feet or so. It was less spectacular, and so perhaps more reasonable, to suppose that the giant leptocephalus was the young of an unknown species that does not grow much after metamorphosis; or that it was a hormonal freak that had failed to become adult. The breeding of marine eels is still in many ways obscure.

It had seemed, though, that the breeding habits of the European freshwater eel, at least, had been established. Then in 1959 Dr Denys Tucker of the British Museum produced a most shocking and ingenious hypothesis. Zoologists had long been surprised at the apparent ability of the European silver eels to swim to the Sargasso; three thousand miles without a single meal, for the gut of the silver eel is very degenerate. (In one famous specimen the anus had disappeared completely.) No other species of eel makes so long a migration. Now, the spawning grounds of the European eel, *Anguilla anguilla*, and the American eel *A. rostrata*, are very close and almost overlap, the American a little more southerly; and the only significant visible differences between American and European eels are in the the number of vertebrae, or of segments in the boneless leptocephali (averaging one hundred and seven in American, one hundred and fourteen in European eels), and in the time spent as leptocephali before metamorphosing. American eels are generally bigger; but this is not a good distinction between species. Tucker suggested that American and European eels are really the same species, and that eggs that develop in the slightly warmer southern spawning grounds have their growth stunted by the heat, and so form fewer vertebrae. (Similar environment-produced changes in the number of vertebrae are known for other fish.) If these stunted leptocephali were then to grow more quickly, they would reach metamorphosis at about twelve months, by which time the currents from the southern Sargasso would have carried them to the American coasts; and if a consequence of not being stunted is to take longer, say two and a half years, before metamorphosis to elvers, this would give time for the non-stunted one-hundred-and-fourteen segment leptocephali to drift over to Europe. If this were so, there would be no need to suppose that any European silver eels at all accomplish the difficult return voyage to the Sargasso. On Tucker's hypothesis, all European eels are really descendants of American eels, and perish futilely in the eastern Atlantic; the eel stock is replenished only from those that make the short migration from American rivers to the Sargasso.

European zoologists have argued against this with almost as much energy as Americans have argued that syphilis really came from Africa. One rather subtle suggestion was made by Dr J. W. Jones of Liverpool; if Tucker were right, there should be very strong evolutionary selective pressures against eels that spawn in the colder northern zone, since none of their progeny will survive, and selection in favour of eels that can recognise the warmer southern zone and spawn there. So after a few million years there should be only eels that spawn in the south. Since this is not so, Jones rejected Tucker's ingenious theory.

But practical tests of Tucker's ideas have proved inconclusive, till very recently; fish that breed only over deep waters cannot be crossed in aquariums and for a long time no really certain differences between the structure of European and American eels were found except for the number of vertebrae; antibody tests, or examination of the chromosomes, failed to distinguish them. (But then, it takes great skill to distinguish man and chimpanzee by these criteria.) Nor had anyone ever caught a European silver eel on its passage to the Sargasso away from coastal waters; though it is not obvious how they could be caught. If they do not feed they cannot be taken with lines; no trawl will easily catch a slender, slippery fish like an eel; and we do not even know where, or at what depth to fish. (No-one has ever caught an American eel on its way to the Sargasso either.)

As one of the less futile gestures of European unity, marine biologists on this side of the Atlantic agreed to make 1979 a year for concentrated research into eel migration. Various ideas were proposed; looking for partly digested European eels in the guts of other deep-sea fishes seemed quite a promising way of avoiding having to catch the eels oneself. In fact, the only recorded observations of European eels in the deep Atlantic was made in 1898, when the Prince of Monaco caught a sperm whale from his yacht off the Azores and found silver eels in its stomach. Tucker, ever ingenious, dismissed these as having just left the rivers of the Azores; but a similar find in mid Atlantic would settle the question.

Another suggested approach is reminiscent of Jewish mythology, in which each skeleton is supposed to contain an indestructible small bone, Luz, from which each body will be resurrected. There are in all fishes very small strong otoliths, more stone than bone, which lie in the fluid-filled inner ear and rest on whichever surface is downmost, and so allow the fish to sense which way is down and which up even in the dark. These do resemble the bone Luz in their durability; even when a fish is eaten whole by another, the otoliths will survive digestion and ultimately fall to the ocean floor. (I cannot guarantee the resurrection.) It was suggested that mud should be dredged up from the possible migration routes and examined under microscopes for eel otoliths to see if any eels died there.

But such a tedious survey may not prove necessary. Appropriately, two Italian biologists, Messrs Comparini and Rodino, proved in 1982 that there really are differences between American and European eels apart from the number of vertebrae; not visible structural differences, but differences in the shape and electric charge of their protein molecules. There are techniques for creating a visible stain wherever proteins that catalyse certain types of reaction are present; if dissolved proteins are put in slots in a starch gel and placed in an electric field, then the protein molecules move through the gel at a rate that depends on their size, shape and electric charge, and when the gel is stained one can see coloured bands that indicate how far different proteins have moved.

Since the structure of proteins is determined by the inherited genes, this method is a very sensitive way of analysing hereditary differences. Comparini and Rodino showed that one such protein, the enzyme malate dehydrogenase, is different in adult American and European eels; it produces bands in different, characteristic positions in starch gels; and the malate dehydrogenase extracted from eel larvae taken from the northern, European spawning grounds in the Sargasso is of the European type, and that from the southern grounds is American. Therefore the two populations are indeed genetically distinct; alas for Tucker's ingenuity.

That is not to say that all the eel's mysteries are elucidated; far from it. The forces that drive the eels on their great journeys are still being sought. Presumably, the European eels have been breeding in the Sargasso since the forces of continental drift started to drive the Americas westwards, and have been gradually increasing the length of their journey. The leptocephali can rely on the surface drift of the Gulf Stream and the North Atlantic Current to carry them across the Atlantic, without steering a course; but they must have some way of knowing when the continent approaches, since they start to change into elvers at about the five-hundred fathom line on the Continental Shelf, though they themselves swim and feed at twenty fathoms or less. It is possible that they can sense the surface waves as they are echoed from the bottom, and respond to the change in echo as the water shallows.

The elvers, arrived at the coast around the beginning of the year, adapt to fresh water over a month or so and then, when the rivers are warm enough (9°C seems to be the critical temperature) swim up the rivers in great shoals, choosing dark nights, keeping a yard or so out from the bank, leaving the water to crawl overland to avoid dams or waterfalls. After a while they become small yellow eels and start to feed. The yellow eels have some migratory abilities; females in particular tend to move upstream in spring and downstream in autumn. And they have a very clear sense of the position of their home stream; yellow eels carried thirty miles overland to another river can return home. Even more strikingly, when they are out of the water they can crawl to the nearest stream; the Swedish biologist, Schaffer, showed that a yellow eel will wriggle determinedly, even uphill and down-wind, to water a hundred yards or further away.

This crawling overland is made possible by the eel's serpentine shape, and its porous slimy scaleless skin through which it can absorb air; also, when eels decide to leave the stream, they fill their gill-pouches with water much as we take a deep breath before plunging. The navigational skills are presumably the same as those of the silver eel; mystery enough. Yellow eels that are trapped in enclosed waters, and know it, delay their late summer metamorphosis to silver, even though they are large enough and old enough. One female, known as Putte, lived in a tank in Salsingborg Museum from 1863 to 1948, when she turned silver and died. Wild eels may stay yellow for thirty years.

Silver eels start their downstream migration in autumn, choosing dark nights in the last quarter of the moon. Pliny said that, in autumn, eels mass themselves together and intertwine themselves into balls; for once, he was right; eel balls several feet across have been seen in modern times, just before the migration of the silver eels starts. Why they do it is still unknown.

The silver eel run is stimulated, it seems, by high waves in the seas to which they run. Eels are astonishingly sensitive to pressure changes; and the Dutch biologist, Deelder, showed that the great runs of silver eels occur in Holland when there is a depression over the Channel or the North Sea (not necessarily over the eels themselves). The storms that the depressions bring set up minute tremors in the earth, from the shock of waves breaking in shallow waters; these can be detected by sensitive seismographs, and by eels. Fishermen have known for a long time that captive silver eels become excited at the time of the great run; they, too, can feel the tremors. (Perhaps yellow eels crawling on land can sense the noise of distant water.) Irish eel-netters used to beat drums to encourage the run to start; the idea was to imitate a thunderstorm, but if it worked the eels took the drums for more distant noises.

Live and smoked eels; jellied and conger eels and elvers

And how do they navigate back to the Sargasso? By the stars, perhaps, till they dive deep; by magnetic sense, like salmon; perhaps by sensing electric fields. Eels are undoubtedly attracted by these last; Polish fishermen use electric currents to drive them into nets. And when salt water, an electrical conductor, flows across the earth's magnetic field, a weak electric current is generated; this has been suggested as the only way an eel can know the direction of flow of a deep ocean current. The sense of smell is highly developed in eels; in experiments, they have detected aromatic alcohols at astonishing dilutions, three molecules to a noseful of water; but this is more likely to help the yellow eels moving to known streams than to aid the silver eels.

Of all these wonderful transmutations, only the yellow eel is of interest to the angler. (Fatty silver eels are better food, but must be netted.) Eel angling is a specialist skill; usually nocturnal, though as Walton knew a hidden eel can be tempted to take a sniggled bait on a warm day in low water. Almost anything can serve as bait; Sir Herbert Maxwell even took eels by fly-fishing, or more accurately hooked them. (The result was an inextricable tangle of eel, fly-line and tree-root.) Even a hook is unnecessary; an old, successful bait is a bunch of worms threaded on a string. A mediaeval variation is a length of sheepgut, knotted at the far end; the eel starts to swallow the gut which the angler then blows up and pulls in.

Of hooked baits, small whitefish are said to be very good, if you live near a lake that has them; or any odorous ledgered bait. There is no delicacy in playing an eel; you need to strike and pull in hard and continuously, with strong tackle, and a wire trace for big ones. Unlike any other fish, eels pull backwards when alarmed; and if they can pull with a purchase on some obstacle, it's nearly hopeless. A stationary eel, pulling, is doing what body-builders call isometric exercises; its muscles are pulling without shortening, and exert their maximum force, far more than they could while swimming.

And when you have landed your eel in the dark, you have further troubles. The experienced lower the eel into a sack, or a deep pail, and cut the line rather than try to unhook. A landed eel wriggles astonishingly. And they are most tenacious of life; beheading an eel only increases its wriggling. The only convenient way to immobilise an eel is to throw a great deal of salt into the bucket. Chilling in a refrigerator also works, if you have one handy.

There remains the minor problem, and mystery, of the poison in the eel's blood. Once again, there is a long history of common knowledge on the subject from fishermen. Gutting eels is quite safe if the skin on your hands is sound, but if eel's blood gets into cuts or scratches they become inflamed and ooze pus; serious poisoning can follow. And again, it was an Italian scientist who first treated the subject seriously: Angelo Mosso, who in 1888 sucked an eel's blood and was "struck by its acrid and burning taste, rather like the venom of a viper". (Those were the heroic days of experimental zoology: modern scientists recognise the taste of venom only in print.) Mosso survived, and injected rabbits and guinea pigs with eel serum (blood liquid with all the cells removed): they died. Later work in France showed that the poison in eel serum is indeed highly toxic; ten microlitres per kilo kills within minutes through paralysis of breathing and heart failure. Taken by mouth, though, it is safe. Heated serum is not poisonous, and protects rabbits against snake venom. Even more oddly, some species are naturally immune to eel serum; frogs and toads, tortoises and vipers, pigeons, chickens, hedgehogs and bats. Few of these normally even see an eel, let alone bathe in its blood. I would like to believe there is a rational explanation for all this.

But eels are not at all poisonous, when cooked. Skinned, sliced and deep-fried in oil; jellied; put into a *matelote*; most delicately, smoked. I have seen smoked eel selling at three pounds the pound; probably worth it. Here is a recipe for the finest smoked eel, from *The Whole Art of Curing, Pickling and Smoking Meat and Fish*, by James Robinson (eighteen years a Practical Curer; London, 1847):
"I should recommend a fine eel of from two to three pounds to be skinned, the head, &c. to be cut off, and split entirely open, laying the bone bare, which should be taken out thoroughly and neatly . . . . Then lay it in salt and water, strong pickle, six hours; take it out, dry it well with a clean cloth, and rub in the following paste, just as much as will cover it all over to the thickness of a sixpence: one large anchovy, beaten well in a mortar; bay salt, 1oz.; brown sugar, ½lb.; saltpetre, 1oz.; sweet lard sufficient to make all into a paste. This done, roll up the fish, beginning with the tail, as tightly as you possibly can, and bind it with a tape; next sew it up into a cloth, leaving the ends bare; put it in the chimney, and let it remain there five or six days in a strong smoke; and after it has got perfectly cold and firm, in two days more you may cut off a slice or two, which should be broiled over a clear fire, and will be remarkably fine."

It seems almost a pity to convert a fish of such abilities to a superior sausage, and frustrate its marvellous powers of navigation.

If they had known of the eel's mysterious journey, the mediaeval naturalists would have made it into some moral allegory; the journey of man's soul, perhaps, that matures for a while in known waters before it returns to the mysterious deeps. Walton, who loved the marvels of the waters, and turned aside to mention the angler-fish and the mighty conger, would have been delighted by the curious mystery. Leigh Hunt, much later, was struck with the strangeness of fish and expressed his astonishment in a memorable sonnet:

> *You strange, astonished-looking, angle-faced*
> *Dreary-mouthed, gaping wretches of the sea,*
> *Gulping salt water everlastingly,*
> *Cold-blooded, though with red your blood be graced,*
> *And mute, though dwellers in the roaring waste;*
> *And you, all shapes beside, that fishy be,*
> *Some round, some flat, some long, all devilry,*

Legless, unloving, infamously chaste –
O scaly, slippery, wet, swift, staring wights,
What is't ye do? What life lead? Eh, dull goggles?
How do you vary your dull days and nights?
How pass your Sundays? Are ye still but joggles
In ceaseless wash? Still nought but gapes, and bites,
And drinks, and stares diversified with boggles?

Hunt knew that was only part of the story; he has another sonnet, which I leave you to find for yourself, giving a fish's view of that extraordinary finless upright creature, man; and a third, inevitably inferior, angel's-eye view reconciling both.

Walton found fish and men alike astonishing, and delightful. There is a state of mind, still flourishing, which rejects curiosity:

Man, dream no more of curious mysteries;
As, what was here before the world was made,
The first Man's life, the state of paradise,
Where heaven is, or hell's eternal shade;
For God's works are like him, all infinite,
And curious search but crafty sin's delight.

This is a grandiloquent rendering of a common theme; by the same Fulke Greville whose own curiosity produced a resonant despair:

Oh wearisome condition of humanity,
Born under one law, to another bound,
Vainly begot, and yet forbidden vanity,
Created sick, commanded to be sound.

To both these melancholy conclusions Walton, and angling, are excellent antidotes; abounding in curious mysteries, and a far from wearisome condition. Some will value the fish more, some the tranquillity; tastes vary, unaccountably. Izaac Walton is the prince of anglers, yet there is no mention of angling, or of his great book, on the stone beneath which he rests in Winchester, above the hidden waters, below the saints and anglers in illuminated glass.

Index